Jennifer is one of those rare authors who [...] journey to wholeness in your life by wri[...] and transparency about her own. She i[...] flaws and faults so that the life of every person [...] read her words can be transformed.

FAWN WEAVER
New York Times and *USA Today* bestselling author

Jennifer has written a relevant, honest, sympathetic, and enlightening book that will deeply touch those secret places inside that seek understanding and truth in the mysterious relationship of marriage. Even more, her vulnerability will give you hope as you journey toward intimacy in your relationship with your husband. I highly recommend this book to young marrieds and to anyone who longs for a stronger marriage.

SALLY CLARKSON
Author of *Own Your Life*

The Unveiled Wife isn't your typical how-to book for wives. It is an invitation to be completely honest with your personal marriage struggles, encouraging you to move beyond them while seeing God's story through them. You will be drawn into Jennifer's story of trials turned redemption and find yourself longing for that in your own life!

RUTH SCHWENK
Speaker, author, and creator of TheBetterMom.com

Jennifer Smith has woven a story of unconditional love with threads of unfathomable grace in the pages of *The Unveiled Wife*. With honesty and vulnerability, she shares her journey of finding true intimacy with both her husband and her Creator. As you encounter her story, you will see your own. You are a woman who is wanted, wooed, and wowed by the ultimate Lover of your soul—Jesus.

KAREN EHMAN
Proverbs 31 Ministries speaker and author of seven books, including *Keep It Shut*

Jennifer Smith bravely shares her wisdom won in the trenches and on the front lines of love and marriage. With raw honesty and transparency, *The Unveiled Wife* pulls back the curtains and shows the struggles and obstacles in real love, sex, and marriage. This book brings hope to the hopeless and light to places of brokenness and despair. If you are looking for the authentic answers to questions for which you may have thought no one had answers, try reading the pages of honesty in *The Unveiled Wife*.

PAM FARREL
Author of forty books, including the bestselling *Men Are Like Waffles—Women Are Like Spaghetti*

As the bride's veil is lifted, her face glows, fully exposed in all her beauty as she awaits her groom to lean in and seal his love with a kiss. The intimacy found in this moment is often lost over time, as the difficulties of marriage cause us to cover up who we really are. Jennifer Smith's book *The Unveiled Wife* will inspire you to live an unveiled life of freedom found in being fully known and loved by God in order to fully know and love your husband.

TRISHA DAVIS
Author of *Beyond Ordinary* and founder of RefineUs.org

Jennifer Smith takes transparency to a sacred level in *The Unveiled Wife*. Her honesty about her unspoken expectations that led to disappointment and her own unconfessed sin that led to near disaster in her life and marriage is without a doubt courageous and admirable. Her journey of humility and surrender, which led to transformation in her life and marriage, will inspire and challenge women to seek a better place in their own lives and marriages.

CRAIG GROSS
Founder of XXXchurch.com and author of Bestsexlifenow.com online video course

Authentic! Honest! Revealing! Surprising! *The Unveiled Wife* is all this and more. If you want to move toward deep intimacy with God *and* with your husband, I highly recommend this amazing book to you! It could change you and your marriage.

LINDA DILLOW
Author of *What's It Like to Be Married to Me?* and co-author of *Passion Pursuit*

With refreshing and fierce honesty, Jennifer takes us behind the veil of some of the most challenging and intimate marriage issues. Whether you are married or single, read this book! *The Unveiled Wife* is the tool women need to help ignite true passion, heal deep hurts, and cultivate thriving marriages that are more beautiful than their weddings.

LARA CASEY
Editor-in-chief of *Southern Weddings* and author of *Make It Happen*

In *The Unveiled Wife*, Jennifer holds nothing back as she humbly unveils her insecurities, struggles, doubts, and fears as a wife and in her marriage. She then captivatingly shows how the Lord transformed her heart. Whether you are married, engaged, or simply planning to marry one day, *The Unveiled Wife* is a must-read that will equip you in your marriage. God's grace and love are evident throughout the pages.

KYLIE BISUTTI
Author of *I'm No Angel*

Jen has the most beautiful and articulate way of opening up her heart and highlighting the redemptive, healing power of Jesus. Her story is intimate and vulnerable; her struggles typify a reality we've all experienced. She's the long-lost sister in Christ who is praying for you, walking with you, and constantly cheering you on in your marriage.

SELENA FREDERICK
Co-creator and writer at FierceMarriage.com

This book not only offers incredible healing for marriages, but it was healing for me as a woman. Jen guides you through the beauty of being vulnerable and transparent with others as well as with your husband. The meaning and value of truly being unveiled and raw with yourself, your husband, and the world is so restorative and leads to such unfathomable intimacy with God. After reading *The Unveiled Wife*, I felt freedom, confidence, and massive amounts of love for me and my husband. I hope every woman and wife can experience the magnificent transformation that comes from being unveiled.

KRISTEN DALTON WOLFE
Miss USA 2009, founder of SheisMore.com, and author of *Rise Up, Princess: 60 Days to Revealing Your Royal Identity*

Jennifer Smith is so authentic and humble as she pulls back the curtain on the first few years of her marriage. For wives who need hope that sex *can* get better, Jennifer points to practical answers to physical problems, but she also shows how our spiritual attitudes are the key to true joy and oneness with our husbands!

SHEILA WRAY GREGOIRE
Blogger at ToLoveHonorandVacuum.com

Hope for today . . . that's what so many women need and what everyone will find as Jennifer takes readers on a journey to a place where so many thought they would never arrive— openness and true intimacy.

LISA JACOBSON
Author of *100 Ways to Love Your Husband* and blogger at Club31Women.com

Lives are radically changed when we surrender our hearts to God's will. *The Unveiled Wife* testifies to that with a beautiful picture of the masterpiece a marriage can be.

DARLENE SCHACHT
Author of *Messy Beautiful Love*

THE

Unveiled

Wife

Embracing Intimacy with God and Your Husband

JENNIFER SMITH

TYNDALE®
MOMENTUM

An Imprint of
Tyndale House Publishers, Inc.

Visit Tyndale online at www.tyndale.com.

Visit Tyndale Momentum online at www.tyndalemomentum.com.

Visit the author's blog at unveiledwife.com.

TYNDALE, *Tyndale Momentum,* and the Tyndale Momentum logo are registered trademarks of Tyndale House Publishers, Inc. Tyndale Momentum is an imprint of Tyndale House Publishers, Inc.

The Unveiled Wife: Embracing Intimacy with God and Your Husband

Designed by Nicole Grimes

Edited by Ginger Kolbaba

Published in association with Loyal Arts Literary Agency, P. O. Box 1414, Bend, Oregon 97709.

Unless otherwise indicated, all Scripture quotations are taken from the *Holy Bible,* New Living Translation, copyright © 1996, 2004, 2007, 2013 by Tyndale House Foundation. Used by permission of Tyndale House Publishers, Inc., Carol Stream, Illinois 60188. All rights reserved.

Scripture quotations marked NIV are taken from the Holy Bible, *New International Version,*® *NIV.*® Copyright © 1973, 1978, 1984, 2011 by Biblica, Inc.® Used by permission of Zondervan. All rights reserved worldwide. www.zondervan.com.

Scripture quotations marked NASB are taken from the New American Standard Bible,® copyright © 1960, 1962, 1963, 1968, 1971, 1972, 1973, 1975, 1977, 1995 by The Lockman Foundation. Used by permission.

Library of Congress Cataloging-in-Publication Data

Smith, Jennifer, date.
    The unveiled wife : embracing intimacy with God and your husband / Jennifer Smith.
      pages cm
    Includes bibliographical references.
    ISBN 978-1-4143-9804-4 (sc)
  1. Marriage—Religious aspects—Christianity.   I. Title.
    BV835.S65 2015
    248.8'435—dc23   2014041085

Printed in the United States of America

21	20	19	18	17	16	15
7	6	5	4	3	2	

To all the people who played a part in God's restoration plan for our marriage. Thank you for allowing God to use you, thank you for your love and encouragement, thank you for your transparency, thank you for crying with us and laughing with us. We love you.

Contents

Foreword

I meet many women facing a crossroads in marriage. Often they don't know where to turn for help. They have read the books, commiserated with friends, and maybe even reached out to a counselor, only to continue to struggle with disappointment. Often these women have lost all hope that things will ever change. After failed attempts at problem solving, many simply choose to give up.

"My husband and I are incompatible. We made a mistake and never should have gotten married."

"He's a wonderful man, but I just don't love him anymore."

"If only I'd known this about him, I never would have married him."

The world is happy to proclaim such women and their husbands mismatched. Devoid of hope, these women begin to consider their options: a lifetime sentence in a lifeless marriage or divorce.

Jennifer Smith and her husband, Aaron, could easily have become one more Christian couple who love the Lord but just couldn't make their marriage work. Instead, they found hope at the crossroads of despair. Without a shred of confidence that they could "fix" their marriage, they threw themselves on the mercy of God, reaffirming a commitment of "till death do us part." Theirs is a love story worthy of Nicholas Sparks, and it happens to be true.

While the specific details of your marriage may differ from Jennifer's, the struggles are likely similar—fading hope for a love that seems irrevocably damaged by sin, selfish choices, and the brokenness of our world. Unfortunately, many wives are giving up on difficult marriages or escaping into fantasy with books like *Fifty Shades of Grey*. Jennifer shares with you how she was tempted to do both. However, the unconditional love of her Savior and her husband invited her to pursue honesty and healing.

Even if they come from strong, Christian backgrounds, almost every couple will face challenges in their intimate relationship. After hearing so many stories from hurting women, I felt the Lord asking me to take a step of faith. In 2012, I left my role as the cohost of the Focus on the Family broadcast to help launch a women's ministry called Authentic Intimacy. My cofounder, Linda Dillow, and I proclaim God's truth about spiritual, emotional, and sexual intimacy. Never in my wildest dreams would I have imagined saying yes to this assignment, especially as the mom of three adolescent boys! Yet God gave me a glimpse of the incredible pain that surrounds the area of intimacy.

That is why I found Jennifer's story so compelling. She holds nothing back, sharing courageously about her insecurities, sexual difficulties, sinfulness, and despair. Her vulnerability is like a mirror, asking each of us to be equally as honest about how we are responding to setbacks and unmet longings within our own marriages.

Every great story involves obstacles that seem impossible to overcome. So does yours. The simple truth expressed through this book is this: "Surely the arm of the LORD is not too short to save, nor his ear too dull to hear" (Isaiah 59:1, NIV).

In my job ministering to women, I regularly see and hear how God does the impossible in our lives when we fully surrender to Him. There is no brokenness that is beyond His healing and no pain beyond His redemption.

May your love story be like Jennifer's, one in which the Lord brings beauty out of ashes!

Dr. Juli Slattery
Psychologist and president of Authentic Intimacy

Introduction

The ebb and flow of life makes for an interesting journey, one that has been full of sorrow and joy, with everything in between, for my husband and me. Most days it all happens simultaneously. The first few years of our marriage were devastating, and my heart broke over the mess we were living in. Marriage was not meeting my needs as I thought it would when I yearned to be a wife. My husband quickly became a source of disappointment, often failing to fulfill me as I thought he should. I harbored a growing anger toward God for not giving me the marriage I had always dreamed of, believing I was entitled to a perfect life because I did all the "right" things for Him.

The greatest trial that overshadowed my husband and me in our first four years of marriage was a sexual problem. In addition to that struggle, the friction of learning how to be one with each other brought other challenges to the surface. I desperately wanted to blame anyone else—mostly my husband—for the problems we faced, in denial that I could be a contributing factor. I was disturbed to find out that *I* fell below par, an image of myself I refused to accept for a long time.

Because we struggled during times of sexual intimacy, I felt inadequate as a woman, as if I were in some way broken. Humiliated,

I doubted God's purpose for my marriage, and I isolated myself from God and from my husband.

In those trying times of conflict and contention, apathy and agony over the desire to separate from my husband, I met God, or perhaps I should say He met me. I thought I had always known Him, yet I struggled in my faith, avoiding Him in anger and feeling miserably stuck in my relationship with Him. Regardless of my rebellion and apparent dissatisfaction, God met me where I was. He taught me who He is, while revealing the intricate details of His design for marriage. In my suffering, God pursued me and carried me to a safe place, an intimate place with Him. As I drew closer to God and allowed Him to show me things about myself that needed attention and change, I learned a few important things about marriage, one of which came through an inspiring message from pastor and author Paul Washer.

> How would you ever learn unconditional love if you were married to someone who met all the conditions? . . . How would you ever learn mercy, patience, long-suffering, or heartfelt compassion if you were married to someone who never failed you? Who was never difficult with you? Who never sinned against you? Who was never slow to acknowledge their sin or ask for forgiveness? How would you ever learn grace to pour out your favor on someone who did not deserve it if you were married to someone who was always deserving of all good things?
>
> The main purpose of marriage is that through your marriage you become conformed to the image of Jesus Christ. . . . You are married to a person who does not meet all the conditions so that you might learn unconditional love. You are married to a person who needs mercy so that you learn to give it. You are married to a person who does not deserve so that you learn to lavishly pour yourself out on a person who does not

respond appropriately. And thus you become like the God you worship![1]

My perspective on marriage changed dramatically after receiving these astounding words. God was teaching me how He could use my experiences in marriage to change me and make me more like Him. He could do the same for my husband. That realization struck me to the core. Marriage serves a greater purpose than I was ever taught growing up. Knowing this gave me hope and faith in my future together with my husband, reconciling and redeeming the love I thought was lost. Only the Lord could overhaul such a broken couple and completely transform us.

Over the last several years, as God continues to transform me and my marriage, I have also learned the value of what it means to be unveiled: to embrace those moments of raw vulnerability in order to draw closer to others in a real way. I have gained a rich understanding of how intimacy is cultivated in relationships by allowing myself to be made known. God gave me the courage to be transparent with Him and with my husband, revealing more about me—my true identity, my heart's desires, and my personal struggles.

God then used the pain from my marriage to birth in me a passion to encourage others in the midst of their hardships. With encouragement from my husband, I created the *Unveiled Wife* blog to share what I was learning about marriage in hopes of inspiring other wives to stand together and affirm one another, and to provide resources to help those in need. As I began blogging, I quickly realized it was as if I had reached up and turned a light on, only to discover that I was not the only one standing there. Where darkness had once overshadowed many of us, the radiant light of Christ exposed the truth that none one of us is truly ever alone.

The message of the unveiled wife is based on 2 Corinthians 3:16-18:

Whenever anyone turns to the Lord, the veil is taken away. Now the Lord is the Spirit, and where the Spirit of the Lord is, there is freedom. And we all, who with unveiled faces contemplate the Lord's glory, are being transformed into his image with ever-increasing glory, which comes from the Lord, who is the Spirit. (NIV)

When anyone turns toward God, the veil is taken away—freedom to be authentic comes and transformation takes place. This is a powerful message that can radically affect marriages for the better. Since advocating for transparency that leads to intimacy in marriage and being open about my own marital issues, one of the greatest responses I have received about UnveiledWife.com is from women saying, "I am not alone."

Simply put, that is why I have written this book. I am a wife who has endured hardship in marriage and can testify to how God turned my mourning into rejoicing.

Shortly after creating *Unveiled Wife*, I felt a divine urge to write my marriage story, specifically recounting the struggle we faced in the bedroom. I was hesitant at first, terrified of exposing my vulnerability. It was also too painful to revisit those uncomfortably difficult times when my marriage almost crumbled. Yet no matter how hard I tried to push from my heart the thought of writing this book, God consistently brought it back to the surface of my heart with a gentle nudge, encouraging me not to be dismayed. He affirmed that my obedience in detailing what He taught me would provide hope and help to other wives. And when I realized that this book could influence women in a real way, I felt responsible, as if I *had* to write it.

Penned throughout these pages are moments from my marriage, events God has used to refine me as a woman and as a wife. I caution you that the majority of the content is regarding sex because that has been our greatest marital struggle by far. (My husband gave me permission to share intimate details about our relationship, and I have had his full support from the beginning.)

As you read my story, you may not be able to understand some of our struggles. (I'm still bewildered with this issue myself.) Or you may read my story and feel astonished that someone else understands the pain you've felt because maybe our experiences are identical. Whether you grasp the weight of our specific issues or can't relate at all, I want you to know my motivation for sharing my story is to help the countless wives who suffer in silence as I did. While your struggles may be different from mine, they may be just as painful. And though sex is a serious issue that I feel compelled to address, I also share the transformation God worked in me and the lessons I learned that have the potential to heal wives and their marriages. I also want to drag several other serious issues into the light—things I know with certainty many women also battle with daily.

I hope my story diminishes the lies that we listen to about being alone in our struggles. Specifically, I hope it unveils the truth about the unmet expectations, imperfections, and insecurities in your own heart as you seek to better your relationship with God and with your spouse.

I admit this book is not intended to be a one-size-fits-all resource, and I am not an expert with a proven method of success to share with you. I am just a wife willing to share my messy life and what God has been teaching me through it. My greatest hope is that you will be empowered and transformed, no matter what season you find yourself in, to live in the freedom of Jesus Christ.

Transformation is an incredible process of positive change. For me, it's a journey of triumph that reflects the awesome power and glory of the gospel. It is the difference between who I was and the God-fearing woman I am becoming. This book is not the sum of my transformation; rather it is just the beginning: the story of a wife saved by God's grace and the extraordinary experience of learning what it means to be unveiled. I'm confident God will use *The Unveiled Wife* to continually speak into your life and encourage you in your walk with God and your marriage.

Dear Lord,

Thank You for the beautiful covenant of marriage, the mystery
of the gospel, and the incredible way marriage—which You
have ingeniously designed so that we may better understand and
experience true intimacy—reflects the love story of Christ. May the
woman reading this book feel You near and know she is not alone.
May You stir a desire in her heart to know You more deeply and
give her the courage to allow herself to be known. May Your Holy
Spirit anoint her as she reads this book and bless her with profound
wisdom and transcending peace as You shape her into Your glorious
image. In Jesus' name, amen!

CHAPTER 1

I Guess This Is the End

S itting in our car's passenger seat, I pulled out my phone
to check Facebook. No immediate or pending actions that
required my attention, yet scrolling through status after status distracted me from reality. My husband, Aaron, and I made
our way through the church parking lot, weaving in and out of
congestion, searching for a parking spot. As soon as Aaron turned
off the engine, we got out of the car and walked to the sanctuary,
synchronized in motion. The morning air was cold, mirroring our
emotion. We continued on autopilot, finding our seats just before
the service began. Though he sat next to me, emotional isolation
left me feeling alone. We didn't say much to each other; the weight
of despair strangled my thoughts, my feelings, and apparently my
speech. I felt as if I were wearing a neon sign that flashed "out of
order," but no one seemed to notice.

I was dying inside, sick with regret over the way my marriage of
almost four years was turning out. My breathing was shallow, a side
effect of the anxiety that relentlessly pummeled my fragile spirit.

Is this it, God? I wondered. *Is this really it?*

My husband had been silent all morning. His eyes reflected
pain and defeat. Bent forward with his elbows resting on his knees,
it looked as if he were wasting away faster than I was.

Why is this happening to us?

I'd never seen my husband so disheartened, and I was clueless about how to respond to him. I wanted to comfort him and say, "Everything is going to be okay," but I felt like I would be lying. We were miles from hope, lost in a world we were not prepared for.

The grief welled up in tears that sat on the rims of my eyes. My husband's head hung low for most of the sermon. As the pastor spoke, I was distracted by negative thoughts. I was angry with God for letting us endure so much hardship, bombarded with familiar and convincing thoughts that I deserved better. I thought following God and being a good Christian guaranteed blessing. I didn't understand that all marriages encounter hardship. So when my marriage didn't meet my expectations, I questioned if I was "good" enough. Doubt stirred in my heart, making me feel inadequate as a Christian and as a wife.

I'm not cut out for this, I thought. As thought after negative thought continued, I turned my frustration toward my husband.

Pretend everything is fine! I can't stand seeing you like this . . . seeing us like this.

I was convinced we would be discussing divorce over lunch.

I wondered how many other people sitting in church that day felt as if they were being buried alive—trapped beneath the weight of a growing pile of dirt. I was ready to make any kind of sacrifice just to survive, yet I wanted to die to escape the pain. I was completely worn out.

When we married, we were adamant that we would face life as a team, committed never to opting out through the "D" word. But already the battle was wearing us down. Unwanted circumstances aroused an unwanted desire for divorce. Contemplating the end of our relationship became an emphatic reality I could not ignore.

Seeing my husband slumped over in church, rotting in despair, made me cringe. In that moment I realized how my actions over the years had taken a toll on his life. I'd been so busy dwelling on my pain that I'd failed to consider how our marital issues were affecting my husband, how *I* was affecting my husband.

That morning as I sat in the church service, I knew this had to be the end of my selfish ways—it had to be or my marriage would die. God finally had my full attention. I knew that only He would have the power to transform me as a wife and heal my broken marriage.

I was humbled, and all I could do was surrender the wreck I'd helped cause. I looked at my husband and prayed, "Lord, please save us. I don't want to divorce this man. Lord, please help us!"

Behind the Veil

1. Unmet expectations became a catalyst for the bitterness growing in my heart toward my husband. I believed he should live up to the standard I held of him in my mind, and when he failed me in any area, discontentment over my *whole* marriage tainted my attitude. In what ways do your unmet expectations affect your attitude toward your husband? Toward God?

2. I thought that as a Christian I had to be perfect so that I wouldn't misrepresent God's gospel to others. Stepping into church and seeing how other people were seemingly so perfect only confirmed my conviction. I didn't want to be the Christian having marital problems, so I pretended my life was great. In reality, smiling on the outside while suffering on the inside never benefits His gospel; it only corrodes my soul. Have you suffered silently in church? If so, what motivated you to hide your pain from others?

3. With all my attention focused on my needs and what would fulfill me, I neglected to consider my husband's needs. I knew what was happening to me, but I figured my husband

could never understand how deeply wounded I felt. In my hurt, I justified that my pain was more important than his. What are some reasons you might consider your pain or frustrations about marriage to be more important than your husband's?

4. "Unwanted circumstances aroused an unwanted desire for divorce." Have you ever contemplated divorce? If so, what unwanted circumstances motivated you to consider the end of your marriage?

CHAPTER 2

Scar Tissue

A fter ushering us into my parents' bedroom, my mom slammed the door shut. My heart raced as she encouraged my brother and sister and me to gather in closely. I sat next to her on her bed while she and my dad raised their voices back and forth through the thin walls of our little home. Both my mom and dad had dominant personalities, so they always fought for the last word during any disagreement. In the midst of their arguing, my mom passed us a pink pastry box with a small doughnut and a half inside. She then urged us kids to split it evenly. Even at age three, I knew the doughnut was just a distraction from the chaos whirling around us. Although I was too young to fully understand the contention between my mom and dad or the exact issues they were arguing about, I remember the uneasy feeling I got in the pit of my stomach when they were at odds with each other.

Soon afterward, my parents divorced. And though I was only four years old, that decision powerfully impacted my life.

Following the divorce, my siblings and I lived with my mother, visiting my father every other weekend. While the outward atmosphere of our family became more peaceful, insecurity took root in my heart. Doubt challenged every relationship I had, whether it was with stepparents, other family members, or friends. I consistently feared that these relationships would tragically end. I overanalyzed every word and action, convinced that I was unattractive, unwanted, and unlovable. The thought of being alone and unloved scared me more than anything else.

The insecurities I faced throughout my childhood only intensified as I grew up and embraced the lies that fed my feelings of unworthiness and the fear that I would be alone. I told myself daily, *I'm too shy, too fat, too clumsy, too stupid, too gross to ever truly be loved.* As the number of ugly thoughts increased and became more descriptive, I became depressed. I struggled to form close relationships because it was difficult to emotionally invest in them. I spent most of my time at home, hiding from the world.

Although my parents divorced, they had been raised knowing God and occasionally talked about Him with my siblings and me. We also went to church most Sundays and every Christmas. To combat the darkness that constantly oppressed me as a young girl, I sought comfort in the God I was learning about. I clung to positive verses I found in the Bible that focused on hopefulness, such as Jeremiah 29:11: "'I know the plans I have for you,' says the LORD. 'They are plans for good and not for disaster, to give you a future and a hope.'" While God always encouraged me through His Word, it was a challenge to confidently believe all He said because I wondered if His Word was really true. I didn't know how to trust the Lord or step into an intimate relationship with Him.

Another way I found to combat the pain of feeling unloved was to watch romantic movies. They allowed me to escape my life as I fantasized about being a character in a happily-ever-after plot.

Throughout junior high and high school, I managed to have a few boyfriends. During those brief relationships, I could never understand why things didn't work out as smoothly as they seemed to in the movies. No matter how hard I tried, those relationships flopped. My desire to get married and experience lasting love propelled me to believe I was the perfect girlfriend and inspired me to do things I thought were romantic. I wrote encouraging letters, gave gifts, scheduled quality time, invited physical touch, and invested in my relationships in any way I thought would make a man fall in love with me. So why did things never work out?

❀   ❀   ❀

Although I did all the kind and thoughtful things I could think of, I knew that I had room to improve in one specific area: communication. It didn't matter if it was communicating with my parents, my friends, or my boyfriend, stress seized my body if I ever had to speak up or confront any issue. With a pounding chest, sweaty palms, and nausea tumbling around my insides, my goal in those moments was self-preservation. I'd think, *How can I make it through this alive?*

With my focus all on me, I was hypersensitive to my emotions and the way I thought I should be treated. If things didn't go my way, I did what I thought necessary to fix the situation. For example, when I felt neglected by my boyfriend, I gave him the silent treatment and the cold shoulder, hoping it was enough to shock him so that he would feel the discomfort, break the silence, and "rescue" me. I considered it to be the man's responsibility to initiate in the relationship. I also assumed the worst was always happening, so I was unable to trust, and on many occasions I twisted my words to draw affirmation from others instead of giving it. I couldn't see that my insecurity gave birth to jealousy, manipulation, and other negative behaviors, making a relationship with me less than appealing. The boyfriends I had during junior high and high school always broke up with me, leaving me to face my greatest fear of being alone.

My experiences never matched or even closely compared to the romantic comedies I enjoyed. The pang of rejection persuaded me to create a barrier in my heart to protect myself from the pain of failed love. I was fragile, with a side of skewed perception—scar tissue from unmet expectations of my family life during childhood. I had no idea what it took to initiate a relationship, let alone maintain one. As a result, I allowed my emotions to take over. They became like the rudder of a ship, directing me where to go, regardless of how irrational my thoughts were. I yearned to matter to others, and I demanded validation for every single feeling I had—something that no one could ever entirely do for me. That never stopped me from wanting it, though.

Rejection hurts. Listening to someone close to me explain why ending our relationship is the best choice really hurts. But despite what I endured through those breakups, I remained hopeful about my future. I prayed often, asking God to prepare and mature the man who would become my husband. I actually had a marriage prayer list that detailed the characteristics I should look for in a husband, as well as those I should exemplify as a future wife. I got it when I attended a Christian youth conference when I was seventeen. The pastor shared the list with a room full of wide-eyed teens—at least I was wide-eyed. His words resonated so much with me that I scribbled them on a piece of paper, folded it, and hid it inside the pages of my Bible, where every so often I pulled it out and reread it.

My Marriage Prayer
- Must be a believer in Christ Jesus (2 Corinthians 6:14-16)
- Must have respect for others as well as himself/myself, especially in purity (1 Thessalonians 4:3)
- Must be motivated in his/my life pursuits (Proverbs 13:4)
- Must not contain any anger (Proverbs 22:24-25)
- Must have strength (1 Corinthians 16:13)
- Must not harbor jealousy (Proverbs 14:30)
- Must be trustworthy (Colossians 3:9-10)
- Must not be a gossiper (Proverbs 26:20)
- Must show discretion (Proverbs 3:21)
- Must pursue wisdom (Proverbs 13:20)
- Must speak good language (Proverbs 17:20; Ephesians 4:29)
- Must not be crabby (Philippians 2:14-15)

- Must have a good reputation (Proverbs 27:2)
- Must be, above all . . . loving (Proverbs 15:17; 1 Corinthians 13)

Desperately wanting to be loved, I prayed and asked God to give me a husband who could look past the scars on my heart, accept me, want me, and unconditionally love me. I needed to feel secure in a relationship, and I believed a godly husband would be able to provide that for me. And yet the scar tissue from my parents' divorce and my failed relationships kept my heart veiled, protected from ever truly allowing myself to be hurt by keeping everyone at a "safe" distance.

Behind the Veil

1. As a child, I never realized how much my parents' divorce affected me. It was not until I matured into adulthood that I could address the ways my parents and their decisions influenced and shaped my character. Reflecting on my past, I can see the wounds it inflicted, stirring up insecurities, as well as an insatiable longing to be loved. In what ways has your parents' relationship shaped your character?

2. As children, we take on behavioral patterns that are direct by-products of the way our parents and other close relatives behave. And as we grow older, we tend to carry those with us. What behaviors—both good and bad—do you have that you recognize as by-products of your childhood?

3. Nobody ever warned me that watching movies and fantasizing would influence the expectations I had about marriage. Nor did anyone explain to me how those expectations, if left unmet, could potentially harm my marriage. Have you ever sought satisfaction and fulfillment

through movies or books? If so, how have they affected your expectations of marriage?

4. My insecurities as a young adult motivated me to live in constant fear. I worried about every detail of my relationships, had a difficult time trusting, and sometimes made assumptions that were just not true. Insecurity in relationships robs us from experiencing true intimacy, the very thing we crave most. In what ways do your insecurities affect your closest relationships?

CHAPTER 3

Is He the One?

As I walked up the driveway, a sense of peace washed over me. It wasn't my house, but it felt like home. The evening sky reflected hues of blue and orange on the back side of white patio chairs flowing out of the garage in neat rows. Bibles, journals, and sweaters saved seats for the high school and college students who were mingling. The walls glowed with bold paint and encouraging posters. Every Monday night for the previous two years, this garage had been my safe haven.

My friends and I called our small group Evergreen. It was one of the many home groups that were available through the church I attended. The people who connected there became my family and helped shape me as a Christian woman by encouraging me to live fully for God and establish moral boundaries. Craig and Corrin, the husband and wife who invited young adults like me over to their home every week, became my mentors, accountability partners, and close companions. I was seventeen years old, a time when I could have wandered in many different directions, but this incredible community influenced me for good, pointing me toward Christ. Evergreen was one of the first places I began to grasp the depths of God's love and my value in His story. Within a few short years, our Bible study, which started out with a few of us meeting in a living room, grew to more than one hundred young adults. New people were joining us every week in that crowded and overflowing garage.

One Monday night in July, while I was saying hello to some friends, my eye was drawn to an unfamiliar face on the other side of the garage. Surrounded by four others, this guy was clearly the center of attention. His 6'1" slender frame, shoulder-length blond hair, and earlobe plugs made him stick out from the crowd. The plugs were round, made of a dark wood, and sat in the center of his stretched earlobes—an accessory that seemed to distinguish him. Something about him intrigued me, but I was too reserved to introduce myself. Glancing his way, I asked a friend if she knew who he was.

"Oh, that's Aaron," she told me.

Although part of me wanted to be in that small group he was chatting with, I didn't know what to say or how to approach them without crushing under the pressure. I figured if he was going to be around for a while, I would get a chance to meet him another time.

Sure enough, Aaron continued to attend on Monday nights, and after a few weeks, he and I officially met. We bumped into each other during study and casually exchanged our names. As we talked briefly, we realized we had many mutual friends, one of whom we both knew from childhood. It was that friend who first invited Aaron to Evergreen.

Within a few weeks , we began seeing more of each other, being cordial on Monday nights, and sometimes hanging out together when a group of our friends went to a show or a late-night stop at Denny's. While I was intimidated by Aaron's intense energy and natural leadership, I also found those qualities refreshing.

Our personalities could not have been more opposite. He was an extrovert—confident, maybe even a little presumptuous, opinionated—and a great conversationalist. I was reserved— a people-pleaser and a poor communicator who kept her opinions to herself.

As we built our friendship, I learned more about Aaron. He had one older brother, he was two years older than me, he was taking college courses, and he delivered pizza part-time. For fun, he sang with a hard-core band, and he volunteered as a youth leader at his church. With each discovery, I grew more intrigued, but what made him most attractive to me was his love for Jesus. It radiated from him. His faith was inspiring, and I wanted to learn more about the passion he had for the Lord.

⊛　⊛　⊛

I had known Aaron only a couple of months when he invited me to volunteer with him as a youth leader. He was always recruiting help, and I knew many of the other leaders serving, which made it easier to take him up on his offer. Working with him in youth ministries became a great opportunity for us to get better acquainted. During our time serving together, I witnessed Aaron's heart for children. He played games with them, prayed for them, and sometimes had the opportunity to preach, encouraging them to live a life dedicated to God. His desire to sacrifice his time and energy for the sake of a younger generation was proof of his maturity and compassion for others—qualities that I found respectable and that were notably on the list I prayed over for my future husband.

I liked Aaron, his style, his confidence, his love for God, and his knowledge of Scripture. Apparently it was obvious just how much I liked him. Friends soon noticed my attraction to Aaron and mentioned the way my cheeks flushed rosy red when his name came up or when he came around. If someone said his name, I blushed. When he walked into the room, I blushed. When he looked at me and said anything, I blushed. This man I was building a strong friendship with also gave me weak knees and butterflies. I loved every minute of our time together.

During the first half of my senior year, apart from school and work, Aaron and I became inseparable. Attending church events and random hangouts together was our norm. We were now close friends, but that's all. While I couldn't help but indirectly express my interest in Aaron, he had not said anything to me about dating.

Sometimes during our Bible studies, I read aloud poems I had written that I felt were inspired by the Lord. My friends knew how passionate I was about lyrical writing and encouraging others through art, and Aaron and I would often talk about those passions. One night after church, I sat on the sanctuary steps chatting with a friend when Aaron approached me, smiling widely.

"Happy birthday," he said and handed me a present. I was just a few days from turning over a milestone: the big eighteen. I was pleasantly surprised that he remembered my birthday was near, yet I was even more shocked by his gift. He didn't stick around to watch me open it, which I appreciated in that moment. I am sure my face was darker red than a beet. I had always wanted to be thought of in a special way, and Aaron had done just that.

I peeled back the wrapping paper to uncover a forest-green journal with a black-and-white image of the Empire State Building centered on it. Opening the heavy, thick journal, I discovered Aaron's scratchy handwriting on the inside cover. My heart thumped as I read:

> *What if there was a God*
> *Who could give you special gifts?*
> *Gifts that could change the world,*
> *Could change people.*
> *What if there was a God who could use you*
> *To do His work,*
> *To show His love,*
> *In a new and wonderful way;*
> *A way that is beautiful and creative,*
> *A way that will make people think.*
> *Would you do it?*

Would you take the gift
And the challenge that comes with it?
You already have.
—AARON SMITH

The words were powerful, awe-inspiring, and deeply thought-ful. I gripped the edges of that journal and held it tightly to my chest. Excusing myself from my friend, I went outside to find Aaron and thank him. I gave him a hug and told him the words he wrote were profound and touched my heart. He just smiled, then wished me a happy birthday again.

There are certain moments that you cherish forever, ones that strike you to the core of who you are, moments that are hard to top. Receiving this gift was one of those for me. I knew Aaron would have no idea what an impact he had made in my life and my writing by saying those few words. He made me feel valued, worthy, loved. I embraced his thoughtful gift and began to con-sider the possibility of Aaron being my husband one day because he made me feel so incredibly secure. My desire was for him to continually feed my soul in this way, hoping that our friendship would turn into a love that would last forever.

Although Aaron's gift did reveal his heart toward me in a beau-tiful way, he never told me how he felt about our relationship going any deeper. Because of that, my insecurities took over and I became unsure of where we were headed. I hoped for more, but we remained only friends.

⊛　⊛　⊛

A big school dance was taking place during the last semester of high school, and a guy from Bible study with whom I'd also been building a friendship expressed interest in being my date for the dance. His pursuit of me caught me off guard, but I liked the feel-ing of being wanted. So I went with him and we had a wonder-ful time together. By the end of the night, he asked me to be his girlfriend. In that moment all I could think about was my longing to escape loneliness, so I said yes.

While dating my new boyfriend, I refocused my time and attention, choosing to let go of other priorities. I stopped volunteering at Aaron's church, and now that I had another guy in my life, I also stopped hanging out with Aaron. Although I missed our friendship, I was excited to be with someone who desired to be with me as more than friends.

As with all my previous relationships, this one didn't last more than a few months, but because I had restructured my time, after the breakup I retreated into isolation. I concentrated on finishing my senior year and working twenty hours a week as a deli clerk at our local grocery store. I kept myself busy to distract myself from the pain of being alone and the uncertainty of what life would be like after I graduated.

In my despair I asked God to help me trust Him to provide a man worth marrying. Then I felt God speak to my heart: *I can't fully trust you with someone else's heart until you trust Me with yours.* I realized God was showing me that I needed to fully rely on Him before I could have a mature relationship with another person. God also longed for me to draw closer to Him. I decided that I needed to let go of my expectations of finding a husband and instead focus on building my character and trusting in the Lord's plan.

Behind the Veil

1. Being around Aaron made me nervous in a good way. I felt flustered in his presence, enamored that I had the opportunity to be his friend. How did you feel when you saw your husband for the first time?

2. The gift Aaron gave me for my eighteenth birthday was one I will cherish forever. It is important for me to remember the

way Aaron expressed his interest in pursuing a relationship with me even as a friend, as it continues to add value to our marriage. In what ways did your husband express his interest in you while being friends? How do those memories add value to your relationship with him now?

3. I impatiently jumped into a relationship, allowing my desire for security to lead my heart instead of waiting and trusting in God. Did impatience or a desire for security make you do something that affected your relationship with your husband while you were just getting to know each other?

CHAPTER 4

"Officially" Dating

⸙

Summer was approaching quickly, along with my joy at grad-
uating. In celebration of the hard work our senior class had
endured together, the high school honored us with a special
dinner at an elegant venue. It was a rite of passage for us as we
ended one chapter in our lives and looked forward to the next.

I had been at the dinner only an hour when I decided to leave
early to stop by a friend's birthday party. Not long after I showed
up, the doorbell rang. A giant stack of ten pizza boxes came float-
ing in. I was surprised to see Aaron delivering the pizza. My heart
jumped, and I didn't hesitate to say hello. His smile made me blush,
and he seemed genuinely happy to see me. Our reunion was brief
since he had to get back to work, but I gave him my new cell phone
number in case he wanted to hang out again. I felt exhilarated.

Aaron and I had been friends for more than a year, but between
our differing schedules and my fleeting dating relationship, we
hadn't seen much of each other for about six months. After we ran
into each other at my friend's birthday party, I hoped to see him
again soon, but I was surprised when he called less than twenty-
four hours later. He invited me to see a movie with him later that
night. Immediately I said yes!

We went to Del Taco before the movie and Krispy Kreme

Doughnuts after—a simple and fun time spent together. Technically this was our first date since it was just the two of us. We had a great night. Things seemed natural between us, and we shared lots of laughter. I was instantly reminded of how good we were at being friends.

For the rest of the summer we hung out, rebuilt our friendship, and got to know each other again. I even went back to volunteering as a youth leader with him, and we began attending Sunday morning service together. It didn't take long for us to become best friends.

We shared the same last name, Smith, so when our friends saw us together all the time, they referred to us as Mr. and Mrs. Smith. We also were asked plenty of times to confirm whether we were dating. I loved the attention we received about our relationship, but I was never too sure what Aaron thought. Until October 9, 2004.

Aaron spent the evening visiting me at my mom's house. When it was time for him to leave, we made small talk as I walked him to his car. He stopped in the street and leaned against a tall brick mailbox next to the curb. I stood on the other side of the mailbox. We stood for a moment in awkward silence as I watched the light of the moon glisten in his eyes.

"So what do you think about us dating?" Aaron finally asked.

My heart nearly flew out of my chest! I was grinning so wide I felt as though my smile couldn't fit on my face, but my nerves kept me from saying a single word.

He grinned. "Are you okay? You look like you're going to explode!"

"Yes!" I nearly yelled.

I had been praying for years that God would give me a man who loved Him and would love me. Aaron had all the characteristics on my prayer list. I knew he was the one. I could see him being my husband, and I envisioned a beautiful life with him. I was eighteen years old when we began dating; Aaron was twenty. We had previously agreed that dating was a serious venture and we would only step into that arena with the intentions of marriage. My dream was coming true! I was thrilled, wide-eyed, and giddy.

Within a week we were holding hands, and the following week, Aaron kissed me on the cheek. Now that we were in an official relationship, we were invested and interested in marriage, which fueled our desires to pursue physical intimacy. Despite having experienced some physical intimacy in past relationships, we were both virgins wanting to save sex until the wedding night. We agreed not to indulge in anything that might compromise our chastity. We avoided spending time alone, when the temptation to engage sexually would be the greatest. We also patiently waited about a month and a half before kissing.

I was wrapped up in love with Aaron; in fact, the whole world could have faded away and I wouldn't have noticed. I wanted to spend as much time with him as I possibly could, and even though we were working, taking college classes, and serving as volunteers at church, we always found time to see each other. We valued our relationship and pursued it as a priority.

Nearly three months into dating, I had an intense urge to tell Aaron exactly how I felt about him. One evening as I got out of his car to go home, I looked at Aaron, beaming with adoration, and summoned the courage to say, "I love you."

He kept his gaze on me while grinning, and in true Aaron fashion, he waited a few seconds for my cheeks to flood bright red, and then replied, "I love you, too."

I was certain then that our decision to be together would soon lead to marriage. I had found someone who would love me through my faults and insecurities. I was confident this was not a fling that would soon die out; rather, we felt compelled and content to be each other's everything!

As our relationship grew, we struggled to enforce the physical boundaries we'd agreed on. Although we never had intercourse, we came close at times and then carried a burden of guilt because of it. We would apologize to each other for our lack of self-control and we would pray together, asking God to forgive us and make us stronger. We tried to make sure we were not out late by ourselves too often, and we spent much of our time hanging out with groups of friends. Keeping each other accountable to stay pure was a huge desire for us. We wanted to exercise self-control and delay gratification until we married, but it wasn't easy.

No matter how much we strived to remain faithful, we often messed up. Our attraction for each other was exciting, and knowing we had boundaries made the temptation even stronger. Kissing Aaron made everything else seem to disappear, including those boundaries we had put in place. We caught ourselves crossing the line many times. The conflict between our cravings and our commitment to remaining obedient to morals was a battle we fought too often. We knew what the Lord expected from us, as well as what our Christian culture expected, but our desires sometimes led us to disregard those expectations. Knowing what we were capable of only fueled our eagerness to get married all the more.

❀   ❀   ❀

Aaron and I dated for a year and a half. In that time we learned even more about each other's character, personality, and faith. We learned the way we respond to different circumstances, how we resolve conflict, and how we love. We never shied away from conversations about important topics like goals, dreams, and marriage. With each passing day I grew deeper in love with Aaron, confident that God had brought us together for an extraordinary purpose. Both of us were committed to discovering God's will for us as a team. We prayed together every day, asking God to guide us in our relationship, to teach us how to work together, to show us what He wanted us to do once we were married, and to keep our goals aligned with His will.

Although we seemed perfect together, at times we still fought and disagreed with each other. Sometimes we even unintentionally hurt each other. I wanted to be Aaron's everything and I wanted him to be my everything. I was convinced that a thriving relationship revolved around this ideal. I wanted to be the center of his world and his reason for living. I wanted him to comfort me, heal me, make me feel pretty, go out of his way to show me how much he loved me, and so much more.

I expected that Aaron would be able to meet my every need. Whenever he failed to do what I thought he should, bitterness built in my heart, ready to detonate at any minute. But I held back, convinced that I needed to hide those emotions so that the hope of marriage was never threatened. As a result, our loving and flourishing relationship was fragile, vulnerable to other negative attacks. Whether personal sin negatively affected our relationship or outside influences discouraged our coming together, we met resistance often. Yet I had great love for Aaron, and I couldn't risk losing his love. Aaron and I talked regularly about our belief that God was orchestrating something big in our relationship. We agreed that Satan would try to steal it, so we would have to hold on tightly.

≫ —— *Behind the Veil* ——→

1. Aaron and I acknowledged our differences and similarities early in our friendship. Sometimes such contrasts can be a huge contributor to contention between couples, while at other times they are the reason couples draw so close. In what ways are you and your husband similar or different? In what ways do those contrasts affect your relationship?

2. Becoming "official" came with trepidation, as I knew it would force Aaron to get to know me in a more intimate way. Yet I was thrilled to know that he felt as strongly about me as I did about him. How did it make you feel when you and your husband became an official couple?

3. Once Aaron and I began dating, to avoid the temptation of sex, we placed boundaries on when and where we spent time together. What kind of boundaries did you have while dating? Did you struggle to keep them? How did you feel if those boundaries were breached?

4. As my relationship with Aaron grew deeper, I assumed he would be the Prince Charming who would rescue me from loneliness—a man who would love me unconditionally, completely fulfill my desires, and satisfy my longing to be valued. In what ways do you expect your husband to be your everything? What dangers are there to having this perspective of your husband?

CHAPTER 5

Hiding My Sin

E very night before Aaron dropped me off at home, we prayed together. If we didn't see each other that day, one of us would call the other right before bed and pray. I appreciated Aaron's willingness to build our relationship on a strong foundation, communicating our thankfulness as well as our longings to the Lord.

Aaron and I had been dating three months when he asked me to pray for him about a specific temptation. He had been struggling with an addiction to pornography for several years. I was shocked, but more by his request than by the actual struggle. I didn't expect Aaron to be so open about something so personal.

Although his addiction to pornography bothered me, I assumed it was every man's battle, especially before marriage. I thought it was something some men needed and assumed that Aaron's desire for it would dissipate after we married. Pornography seemed inescapable, so it made sense that Aaron had been exposed to and was struggling with it. Although Aaron's secret never diminished my love for him, I was ignorant about the issue, and I did not fully grasp how to approach his struggle other than through prayer.

I was thankful he had enough integrity to be transparent about his battle with pornography, so I told myself what I wanted to hear: *It isn't really a problem and it will go away as soon as we're married.* Knowing that the man I loved was a slave to his addiction grieved me, but it seemed easier and far more comfortable to trust he was working it out on his own than to try to hold him accountable.

Plus I had my own issues to deal with, and part of me did not want the reciprocal accountability. I had an image to uphold, or so I thought. I definitely wasn't willing to be as honest with myself or others as Aaron was with me.

The truth was that I had also been exposed to pornography at a young age and at various times throughout childhood. As a curious child, I had stumbled upon a few sexually explicit materials, including romance novels, magazines, and movies on cable. Sometimes images of nude women littered the gutter my friends and I walked by on our way home from school, giving us kids something to chuckle about. We had no concept of how it was polluting more than just the streets. Other times I intentionally searched for it in places I thought it might be hiding, such as on certain television channels or tucked away in relatives' bathroom drawers. As I grew older, the images that had become seared into my mind caused deep shame and remorse. While I was not addicted to pornography, I became susceptible once those pathways were forged in my brain.

When I did come across pornography, it enticed me so strongly that I allowed my mind to dwell on it. Based on what I saw, my imagination would create stories, scenarios that sent a rush of good feelings throughout my body. Fabricating a fantasy world became my vice, filling me with shame. And it was during those moments of intense shame that I felt loneliest. At times I desperately wanted to tell someone my secrets, to ask for help to overcome the temptations, but I was fearful, terrified of being judged. Plus, I didn't want to tarnish God's reputation, believing my sin had more power to turn people away from God than the power His story and grace had to draw them in.

So when Aaron told me about his struggle, I listened but didn't share my own struggles with him. I justified my silence, unwilling to be that transparent with another person, even though what I wanted most was a truly intimate relationship. I wanted to be known, unveiled, but I didn't know how to let down the barriers that I thought were there to protect me from getting hurt.

I knew drawing close to God would be the only way to gain freedom. Praying for each other every night either in person or over the phone was our way of doing that. Praying together helped us focus on God's will and kept us accountable to our faith, reminding us daily that our relationship would always take second place to our first priority: God.

As much as I prayed with Aaron, I also personally approached God through prayer. I thanked Him for Aaron's honesty and prayed for freedom from sin, but many times I felt unworthy to talk to Him because of all that I was unwilling to confess. I only ever scraped the surface of my heart when praying, resisting going to the deep places with God. I believed in faith that Aaron would be set free from his addiction and that God had a perfect plan for our relationship, but there were so many more layers separating my true heart from God. Although I too wanted to be set free from my sin, I was not willing to address any of it before God. I was living in denial, actively ignoring the very issues hurting me the most. I convinced myself that my struggles were little, and as long as no one else knew what I was dealing with, I would be fine.

≫ ——— *Behind the Veil* ———➤

1. Looking back now, I wish I'd had the courage to seek more help with my sin of lust, and I wish I had taken Aaron's addiction to pornography more seriously. The consequences of our personal transgressions caught up with us in our intimate relationship as husband and wife. The pain of guilt

and the damage we caused each other planted doubt and distrust in both of our hearts. Was there anything in your life or your husband's life that was unveiled while dating that negatively affected your relationship after you got married?

2. Being transparent about personal struggles requires humility, courage, and an understanding of why it's important to be unveiled. In what ways was your husband transparent with you before you married? Were you transparent with him or did you choose to withhold? Why?

3. Studies show that many people are first exposed to pornography by the time they're eight or nine.[2] One study even suggests exposure as young as five or six.[3] Have you ever struggled with pornography? If so, how old were you when you first started searching for it, and how did it make you feel? Do you or your husband struggle with it today?

CHAPTER 6

Engaged

Sitting at the computer in Aaron's parents' home, I watched a slideshow of family photos fade on and off the screen. Aaron broke my concentration when he called me into his room and invited me to sit next to him on his bed. Aaron held his Bible firmly, a hand-me-down he had received from his father a few years before. He had sewn a denim cover for it, similar to the one I had sewn to protect mine, a coincidence that made me smile.

From the inside of his Bible cover, Aaron pulled out a handful of small pieces of paper, tattered and worn from being clutched many times, and handed them to me to read. The dates were the first thing to catch my attention: each paper was dated at least two years earlier. The realization that Aaron and I had been dating for a year and a half popped into my mind. I couldn't believe how fast time had passed. Each paper was filled with Aaron's scratchy writing. They were prayers Aaron had written and clung on to, desires of his heart.

By the time I had read the third prayer, my own tender heart felt overwhelming love for the man sitting next to me. Each prayer was a plea, asking God to prepare him and his future wife for each other, and to bring them together at the right time. He revealed his longing to be married and asked God to give him the patience to wait for the woman who would be his wife.

Since writing those prayers when he was barely eighteen years old, Aaron, now twenty-two, had not dated anyone except me. After reading them, I met Aaron's teary gaze. With a soft voice, he confidently claimed that I was the answer to his prayers. My heart leaped as I understood how much he truly loved me. Aaron continued with a most genuine proposal, inviting me to become his bride. He told me life would not always be easy, but that he would always trust in God and lead me to do the same. Then he gave me a tiny black box to open. Inside sat my ring, my security, my future.

I was speechless.

Aaron slid the ring onto my finger, and his warm hands embraced mine. "Can I pray with my fiancée?"

I laughed and cried as I pushed forth a simple yes. Bowing our heads in thankfulness, we prayed for our marriage-to-be.

⊕　⊕　⊕

As amazing as that moment was for me, when I left Aaron's house, I was immediately filled with fear. I dreaded telling my mom and stepdad that we were moving forward in our relationship. A few weeks earlier, Aaron and I had had conversations with our parents about the idea of marriage and missionary work, explaining our desire to be a team for God and travel the world to tell others the gospel. My dad and stepmom, as well as Aaron's parents, were thrilled about our decision to marry. However, my mom and step-dad did not see eye to eye with us. Since my life plan didn't match their long-standing expectations for my future, the conversation ended on a less-than-harmonious note. My parents reminded me that I was only twenty years old and that they wanted me to finish college, get a degree, and fulfill my potential in a secure career.

Although I was diligent in school, I did not feel settled in the direction it was taking me, and I felt an overwhelming desire to use my time in other ways, like gaining experience through traveling abroad. I also knew school was something I could always pursue later.

Ideally Aaron and I both wanted my mom and stepdad's support for the decisions we made, but our expectations were drastically different from theirs. And the burden this resistance placed on me was nearly unbearable.

I was a people-pleaser—especially a parent-pleaser. From a young age I yearned for my mother's approval and to know she was proud of me. Although many times my mom did satisfy this yearning, it remained a constant need, especially when I had to make the most crucial decisions. I knew she wanted the best for me because she told me that often. Unfortunately, our definitions of "best" were just not in agreement this time.

My mom, stepdad, Aaron, and I were all emotionally invested in my life, and knowing my decision would affect everyone caused me a lot of stress.

I waited until the following morning to break the news. The moment was filled with awkward emotion. I could tell they were hurting by the sadness in their eyes, but I stood firm in my decision to marry the love of my life. While becoming a wife was significant to me, the agony of believing I was disappointing those who had sacrificed so much for me crippled my confidence. Their lack of support made me doubt whether I was making the right decision.

A month after our engagement, the sting of our plans still upset my mom and stepdad. At one point, I even attempted to break up with Aaron to relieve the pressure. I told him one Sunday after church that I was not happy and couldn't marry him. I knew I was hurting him, but I didn't know how else to handle the situation. Near the end of our conversation, however, I realized my love for Aaron outweighed my other important relationships. I did not want to give up on him, I just wanted the resistance against our relationship to stop. Aaron held my hand and we reaffirmed that we must hold on tight to the love that we shared.

I spent serious time in prayer, begging God to bring peace to my family. I asked God to guide me and help me do what was necessary to please only Him. I trusted God to give each of us understanding about the future, and I faithfully believed in God's best for my life. Within a week of my intentional prayer for peace, my mom relinquished her fight for my future and gave me the support I desperately wanted from her. God heard my prayer and He moved miraculously in all of us.

My engagement to Aaron lasted a brief six months. In that time we not only prepared for every detail of our wedding, we also invested in our future through premarital counseling. We identified our love languages and talked about some of our expectations of each other. Aaron mentioned how he hoped I would follow him and allow him to lead, as well as to keep myself healthy well into old age. I responded by sharing how I hoped he would work diligently, assume the responsibility to take out the trash, and that he, too, would try to remain healthy.

We laughed our way through many conversations about marriage, completely unaware of the realities of married life. As much as we shared our expectations, we only scratched the surface. Many of my expectations, such as what would happen in the bedroom, remained tucked away. I had high hopes for a great sex life. And based on our physical attraction to each other, I could not fathom anything going awry. As much as I anticipated consummating our vows, a part of me was terrified about being so bare—physically and emotionally—before my husband.

>>————— *Behind the Veil* —————▶

1. I thought I wanted a theatrical proposal, an over-the-top performance in which my future husband would prove his love with daring gestures. The twist I never saw coming, though, was the moment of vulnerability that led Aaron

to show me the tattered papers on which his prayers were recorded, indicating his desire for me long before he even met me and illustrating how the power of God worked to bring us together. I appreciated how thoughtful and genuine his proposal was, and it satisfied my heart completely. What are some of the details of your proposal? Did it meet your expectations or did it surprise you?

2. I value my parents and their hopes for my life. Although they wanted only the best for me, it became a challenge to reconcile our different feelings about my upcoming marriage. Their resistance caused me to doubt my decision, which almost convinced me to end my engagement. In what ways did you and your fiancé encounter resistance to your relationship? How did you overcome it?

3. My expectations for marriage were based on observations I had made growing up. While there is nothing wrong with having expectations, it is important to evaluate whether or not they are realistic. It's equally important to respond with grace when those expectations are not met. What were some of your expectations for marriage, especially your sex life?

4. Premarital counseling was a great opportunity to really think about our life together as husband and wife. Unfortunately, Aaron and I approached our sessions lightheartedly, convinced our love would be enough to carry us through a lifetime of marital bliss. I wish we had invested more time in each counseling session and intentionally considered the importance of such a safe environment to discuss intimate matters prior to marriage. Did you go through premarital counseling? If so, in what ways do you think it did or did not prepare you as a wife? What areas of marriage do you wish you had been counseled on?

CHAPTER 7

The Wedding

❧

I awoke early on January 6, 2007, with a smile from ear to ear. I was getting married!

Before the house began to stir in excitement, I arose, got dressed, and snuck out to the hair salon to start step one of the beautification process. I'd decided to get extensions to add body to my fine hair. The extensions were tracks that were glued in from the top to the bottom of my scalp. Unfortunately, as my hairdresser tried to place my veil, we realized the tracks were getting in the way. She worked for another ten minutes pinning my veil as tightly as she could. After we reached a point where the veil seemed to stay, I thanked her and jumped into the car to make my way back home.

Within seconds of heading down the road, overwhelmed by all that would happen that day, I burst into tears, bawling like a baby. I had assumed this day would be emotional, yet I didn't expect it to start with my hair. I probably looked like a runaway bride, crying as I raced down the freeway with my veil slipping from my head. Once I arrived home, I ran straight upstairs to the bathroom. With only a few hours before the wedding, I began to tear down my hairdo in a panic.

Hearing my cries, my mom rushed in. "What are you doing?"

As I explained my veil situation, my mom stood by my side and tried to help as much as she could, encouraging me that everything would turn out all right. We were able to fix my hair, and somehow we firmly placed the veil just as I had imagined it. I was learning that life requires flexibility, more so on wedding days.

I drove by myself to the church to complete my transformation. As soon as I got out of the car, I ran into the church, afraid that my veil would fly off my head again since the Santa Ana winds were in town, adding more drama to the day. I entered the bride's quarters; a few of my bridesmaids were already there and beaming with enthusiasm. Soon almost twenty family members and friends were packed in that small room, all of them willing to help wherever needed.

Everything was happening rapidly. As the guests began to arrive and my bridesmaids hustled around the room getting themselves ready, someone knocked at the door. My dad wanted to give me a quick hug, but at first glance we both started to cry.

With my arms wrapped tightly around him, I whispered in his ear, "I can't believe I'm going to be married!"

He was speechless, but I knew what he was thinking: His little girl, who had just turned twenty-one, was now about to leap into marriage.

"I love you so much!" he finally said. Looking at the full-grown woman before him, he tilted his head in admiration. I could tell he was wondering how I'd matured so quickly. He gave me one more giant smile and then exited the room. I ran to the mirror to check on my makeup, now that I'd been crying. Other than my red eyes, everything was perfect. I stood in front of my reflection, waiting to be called downstairs. My mom stood by my side, checking and double-checking that I had everything I needed, randomly fluffing out my dress or straightening the ends of my veil.

I mentioned to her how nervous I felt about walking down the aisle in front of everyone, and how nervous I was about being a wife. She grabbed my hand, squeezed tightly, and reassured me that everything was going to be all right and that no matter what, she and my stepdad would be there for me. After taking one more glance in the mirror, I headed downstairs.

⊛   ⊛   ⊛

As I stood in the hall, patiently waiting for my cue to enter the sanctuary, I grasped my stepdad's arm. His eyes were filled with tears, revealing emotions he was usually better at hiding. In that moment I thanked God for providing such a caring and selfless man to love my mom and receive her children as his own, to receive me as his daughter.

The piano music filled the sanctuary and announced my entrance. My friend Brad was performing a song he and Aaron had composed just for me, titled "My Living Prayer." The significance of every word motivated my shy self to make my appearance. I began walking down the aisle, concentrating on my balance, holding on to my stepdad and my dad for support. I was blessed to walk down arm-in-arm with both my dads, who handed me off to the man who would become my husband.

Climbing the sanctuary stairs in my embroidered gown and champagne heels, I thought about one of the first movies that impressed a desire for true love upon my heart. I was Cinderella, saved from despair by my Prince Charming after being raised in a family who had struggled to grasp emotional peace and financial freedom. Those steps I stood on to share my vows were the same steps I had sat on when Aaron had given me that beautiful birthday gift nearly three years before. He had captured part of my heart then, but now I was able to give him all of it. He would be the most important person in my life, the one with the most power to influence and affect me.

As nervous as I had been walking into the sanctuary, most of my fears subsided once Aaron held my hand. His presence alone brought both peace and calmness. I give him most of the credit, but our pastor deserves a small percentage of acknowledgment since he wore one of the most distracting ties I had ever seen: a dark green leafy pattern with hidden characters from Winnie the Pooh staring at me, congratulating me with smiles. I had to suppress my laughter and take the pastor seriously when he walked us through Communion.

Everything that occurred during our wedding ceremony represented the love Aaron and I shared for each other and for God—from the slideshow that played photos of us growing up and meeting each other to the praise music we had chosen for the ceremony to the vows we made to the candles we used to light a single flame signifying ultimate unity. It was one of my happiest moments, and Aaron and I made sure to give God all the glory! I was blessed to see so many people celebrating such an important milestone with us.

When the pastor introduced us as Mr. and Mrs. Smith, I was incredibly happy. I was on top of the world, standing next to my best friend, knowing we were officially and forever a couple. My new life, my perfect life—the one I'd waited for and dreamed of—was now beginning.

>> ———— *Behind the Veil* ————→

1. Whether a wedding takes place in a church, in a home, in the openness of nature, or simply in a court office, it is a celebration and a witnessed commitment of two becoming one. What are some standout memories of your wedding day?

2. Life requires flexibility, weddings require flexibility, and marriage requires flexibility. In what ways have you encountered a need to be flexible? And how does your perspective or attitude contribute to your ability to be flexible in these moments?

3. Becoming a wife was a dream come true for me. I had longed to have a man intimately know and unconditionally love me. When I heard the pastor announce to the world that we were husband and wife, I beamed with incredible joy. Think back to that moment just after you committed your vows to your husband. How did you feel, knowing you had just become a wife?

CHAPTER 8

Trouble in Paradise

O
ur wedding party followed us outside for a grand good-
bye. Dusk was settling, and Aaron and I were eager to
start on our honeymoon. We jumped inside our little red
Jetta, on which someone had written "Just Married!" with a bold
white marker. Thank goodness for tinted windows! We waved to
everyone who had shown up to support us and nestled in for a two-
hour drive that would take us to a small hideaway town tucked into
the hills of San Diego County.

As our journey began as Mr. and Mrs. Smith, we could not stop
talking about all we had experienced that day. Aaron and I took turns
sharing favorite parts of our wedding celebration, chatting about our
perspectives from the altar and laughing over the parts that didn't
quite meet our expectations. Thirty minutes or so into our trip, I
asked Aaron to pull over and get my jacket out of the trunk. I had
kept my wedding dress on for the trip, and its strapless neckline was
leaving me chilly. I would have just turned up the heater, but I didn't
want my husband to suffocate from the heat just because I was cold.
(While dating, we'd discovered that our ideas of the "perfect" tem-
perature were the opposite. Aaron always ran hot; I always ran cold.)

He stopped, went to the trunk, and then yelled up to the front
that my bag wasn't there.

"What?" Disbelief coated my voice as panic shot through me.

Aaron jumped back into the driver's seat, disappointment written over his face. "Your bag isn't in the back. None of your stuff is there."

Tears swelled up in my eyes and ran down my cheeks. This day had been the most exciting, yet exhausting, of my life. My emotions were high. Plus I felt panicked that we were already going to be late for our lodging check-in—not to mention feeling insanely nervous over the ever-looming thought of having sex for the first time. Now both of my bags were missing!

One bag was just my clothes, but the other one was a magic bag filled with flavored lubricants, sexy games, and lingerie, which I had received at my bachelorette party. I didn't know what I would need for my first experience with sex, so I had packed most of the items in that bag to build my confidence and guide me through my most vulnerable night.

I grabbed my phone and hit speed dial, taking a deep breath to calm down.

My stepdad answered with an endearment, "You can't change your mind now, Jen Jen!"

I tried to laugh and sound natural. "Actually I need some help." Holding back tears of embarrassment, I explained, "This morning I put my bags in your car and drove to the church, and, well, they never made it to *my* car."

He promised he would come right away, and we waited in a parking lot off the I-15 freeway for another forty minutes while my stepdad came to the rescue. But when he got out of his car, he had only one bag in his hand—the bag with my clothes. As I caught Aaron's look, humiliation flooded my face as I realized my bag of "tricks" had accidentally been left by the front door of my mom's house.

I really hope nobody digs through it before I get back, I thought.

Despite my overwhelming disappointment, I thanked my stepdad for his help, and then Aaron and I were back on the road.

❀   ❀   ❀

We pulled up to the bed-and-breakfast an hour and a half late. Aaron's parents had surprised us with a paid two-night stay, so we weren't sure what to expect. Unfamiliar with the area, Aaron rolled down his window to ask a passerby for directions. The man was walking between two properties that were separated by a small hedge of green bushes. Pointing to the house in front of us, Aaron asked, "Excuse me, is that where we would check in for the bed-and-breakfast?"

Without a kind smile or even lifting his head the man replied, "Not unless you want to sleep in my house tonight." He pointed toward the house on the left and said, "It's the place next door."

We parked our car where the man had directed and grabbed our bags. Upon entering, we were welcomed by the same man we had unofficially met outside. He was the owner of the B and B and seemed perturbed by our tardiness, judging by the way he gave us a quick tour of the premises.

Our suite was smaller than we thought it would be. The queen-size bed took up the majority of space, leaving only about a foot and a half around each side for us to walk. Every wall was plastered with eggshell-colored wallpaper with a light mauve floral print running from the floor to the ceiling. The floral pattern seemed to be the theme for our suite, covering the upholstery on two ancient chairs, set in frames as art, and woven into the fabric of our comforter. The same mauve covered the ceiling and was painted on a brick fireplace that sat in front of our bed. A chandelier hung in the corner of the room, reflecting shiny light off the wallpaper and white-laced window drapes. Regardless of the room's appearance, which made us laugh as it transported us back in time, my husband and I were beginning our journey together, ready to enjoy life as one.

Now alone, Aaron and I jumped playfully into bed. With most of my knowledge about sex coming from romantic comedies and brief conversations with my mom about the consequences of premarital sex, I had no idea what we were really in for. Aaron gently kissed me, leading us into an intimate time of exploring each other's bodies. We were wrapped in each other's arms, more vulnerable than either of us had ever been.

As wonderful as it was, however, we struggled through awkward position after awkward position trying to find one that worked. But nothing seemed to, as pain inflamed my lower region. Although a part of me just wanted to push through the uncomfortable feelings, I couldn't. They were not just uncomfortable, they were excruciating.

Tears began to roll down the sides of my face, landing on my husband's shoulder. He was patient with me and held me close as he whispered, "It's okay."

We lay there together for a few moments, overwhelmed by the exhausting day. Although I craved to be next to Aaron, comforted by his love, I forced myself to get up. I went to the bathroom and filled the bathtub. As I sat in the steaming hot water, I thought about how inadequate I felt, and my tears continued to flow.

I didn't expect to have that feeling as a wife, let alone to have it barrage me on my first night of marriage. I was not mentally or emotionally prepared for my body to malfunction during sex. I didn't know what to do.

The door squeaked open. Aaron stuck his head in and told me again that everything would be okay, that he wasn't upset, and that he never would be. He said that he would be there with me even if having sex took us years to figure out, but then he laughed, convinced that it wouldn't take more than a few days. We got back into bed, holding each other as we fell asleep.

❀　❀　❀

Waking up the next morning seemed dreamlike. For an instant I forgot where I was but quickly realized that the man lying next to me was now my husband. Joy flooded my heart as I curled up next to him, taking advantage of the opportunity to cuddle before breakfast. A wonderful aroma wafted up from the kitchen and filled our room, causing my stomach to stir. I woke Aaron with soft kisses all over his face. We didn't try sex again that morning, with the memories of the previous night still in my mind. Instead we ventured out of our room to enjoy the day.

The Santa Ana winds were still whirling around us. January was cold enough up in the higher elevation of Southern California, and these winds made it shockingly worse. We tried walking on Main Street, but the weather made it nearly impossible. It seemed like we were in a ghost town. We headed back to our suite for our couples massage, but that too was less than impressive. The older hands of my masseuse felt like sandpaper on my wind-chapped skin. I shook off my unmet expectations for the massage and eagerly awaited our horse-drawn carriage ride, another reminder of my life mirroring Cinderella's. However, our carriage ride lacked a certain royal appeal.

The crisp cold and high winds stirred a specific aroma in the air, a stench that made our eyes squint. If it wasn't bad enough that we could not escape the scent of horse manure, the kind driver handed us a blanket to encourage us to keep warm, which was covered in animal hair and intensified the smell that made my stomach churn. After only a few minutes of our romantic ride, we insisted the driver cut our trip short and drop us off for our dinner reservations. My food that night, Italian baked ziti, was the highlight of our entire honeymoon! I would have also considered the personal Jacuzzi that sat on the porch of our suite as a favorite memory; however, Aaron and I both received chemical burns from the over-treated water, a reaction that left us with burning, itching skin for nearly three weeks!

Although these events frustrated us at the time—and fortunately were a source of humor later on—they were nothing compared to the one thing we craved most and that frustrated us most: consummating our marriage. Our sexual experiences were not unfolding as we had hoped. But we were still determined to be as

close to each other as we could. We snuggled in bed, watched movies, gave each other relaxing massages, and basked in each other's
company. Spending so much time in our little suite gave us ample
opportunity to attempt sex a few more times. Each time, however,
the pain I experienced was unbearable.

I knew Aaron had to be frustrated, but he remained patient with
me and quick to comfort me as much as he could. Determined
to experience the ecstasy of love, we found other ways to pleasure
each other. And while we had some good moments, the shadow
of unmet expectations hung over the honeymoon and our newly
formed marriage.

Up until the wedding night, I had assumed we would experience extreme closeness by having sex. I longed to fulfill the one
aspect of our relationship that we had kept guarded. And although
I had heard stories of other virgins encountering pain during sex,
I was sure that *if* I felt anything painful, it would be only a small
amount of discomfort. My expectations had led me to believe that
sex wouldn't be nearly as difficult as it actually was. I tried to accept
my husband's continued support and words of encouragement,
but doing so was a challenge. I listened to Aaron tell me that he
was not mad and that we would be able to have great sex soon, but
my insecurities seemed to yell louder, telling me that I had already
failed my husband. The ideal I had clung to since childhood, my
fairy-tale marriage, already seemed to be in trouble. This wasn't the
way it was supposed to work out.

>> ———————— *Behind the Veil* ————————>

1. My husband and I were virgins when we married. Although
   we desired to fulfill each other completely on that first
   night together, the truth was that we had no clue what we
   were doing. Sex might be a natural occurrence, but I now
   believe it gets better over time as a husband and wife get to

know each other in a profoundly deep way. Were you and your husband virgins when you married? How did your experiences or lack of experience affect your wedding night?

2. Every couple encounters a different type of honeymoon, and some do not have one at all. In our case we had a brief and unsatisfying adventure. We promised to make up for it throughout our marriage as often as we could by going on mini-adventures. Did you enjoy your honeymoon? What were some highlights you and your husband still talk about?

3. I felt physical pain during sex, a sensation that did not let up any time we tried to pursue intimacy. This was not an issue we had discussed in our premarital counseling, nor was sex an easy thing to talk about with my family or friends. I did not think we would encounter such a unique trial, but we did and it affected us in many ways—from our attitudes to the way we communicated and so much more. Did you encounter any physical or emotional pain on that first night of your marriage? How did you respond to the situation?

CHAPTER 9
It's My Fault

I flipped my pillow around to get comfortable. The room was pitch black, and besides the hum of a bedside fan spinning to help Aaron fall asleep, it was quiet. We had been husband and wife only a few short weeks, and we still had been unable to fully enjoy sex. As I settled in and closed my eyes, I felt my husband's warm hand caress my arm. He leaned over and kissed me gently on my cheek. Without saying a word he called my name and invited me to join him. Despite the last few weeks of failed attempts, we remained hopeful about consummating our marriage.

Aaron did everything right. I felt safe in his arms, I knew he loved me and was passionately pursuing me. What I couldn't explain was how we could engage in closeness for more than an hour and still not be able to experience the satisfaction of intercourse. Whenever we tried, tears streamed down my face, a response to the physical agony. My body was in pain, my heart was shattered. It felt as if I were tied to a bungee cord and I had just reached the end of my free fall. The force of being pulled back introspectively took my breath away. Echoes of self-concern and self-condemnation repeated in my mind: *It's all my fault. It is my fault that we're having issues, because it's my body that will not cooperate.*

Carrying the guilt of believing I was at fault was a weight I was not strong enough to bear. It crippled me in my marriage and in my faith. I chose not to pursue my husband in a romantic way, and when he initiated, I often responded with an excuse, uninterested in feeling any sort of pain. Aaron and I still prayed together, especially over this major marital burden, but it was difficult for me to believe that the pain was going to end one day. Depression pressed in on me, and in my weakness, I retreated, isolating myself from Aaron. I hated being consumed by those feelings because I couldn't just apologize and change. It was never a choice to change, so every time we engaged in sex I was reminded of my brokenness, my fault. I kept my feelings of failure to myself, hoping that my husband would not confirm any of it, for if he did, I could only imagine our marriage ending.

We had expected to solve the mystery of why intercourse seemed impossible within a few days after the wedding, yet it remained unsolved. I knew before we married that it was normal for virgins to experience discomfort, pain, or even bleeding during sex. I understood that every woman's body is unique and yes, I was aware that the hymen could tear causing minimal to extreme pain. I had heard stories of some wives encountering pain during intercourse, and with every week that went by without successfully experiencing intercourse, I became more worried and fearful. I began to assume that maybe we were physically incompatible. I doubted whether our love was real and whether God truly had destined us for each other. The uncertainty confused me, making it even more difficult to be aroused in the times we pursued sexual intimacy.

I was mortified that we could not enjoy sex. I feared that my husband, my best friend, would find fault with me as I had. Nothing on which I'd based my expectations—the romantic movies I'd watched and compared my marriage to, the fairy-tale dreams of happily ever after—included rejection. How long would Aaron stay with me if we couldn't fully experience sexual pleasure? I would be devastated. Since it had been only a few weeks since we'd said "I do," I tried encouraging myself by acknowledging the fact that we had the rest of our lives to improve this area. Realizing my dramatic doubts may have been coming on too strong, too soon, I tried to snap out of it. I wanted to convince myself that sex was new to us, and it would take time to adjust.

As the weeks went by, our "trying" became even more disappointing, and the pain I experienced was wearing me down. No matter how upset I became in those moments, Aaron would gently wrap me in his arms and whisper, "It's okay." He would say things like, "I'm having fun with you" or "Let's just explore each other's bodies." He would stop if he could sense I was tensing up and ask if we could continue later or the following night. Despite the doubt that filled my mind about our relationship, Aaron's actions proved to me that I had a special husband—a man who would stay in a sexless relationship and still find the strength to comfort and love his wife, a man who had the willingness to endure through hardship.

Aaron occasionally mentioned his frustrations over our sex life, but it was always a precursor to encouraging me to seek help, to see a doctor, or to talk to someone who could give us some answers. Other times he voiced his concerns indirectly through prayer. Although I knew our inability to have satisfying sex must have upset him, he never responded to my lack of performance in anger, resentment, or bitterness. I was a fortunate wife married to a patient man.

I should have been thankful for the gift of the husband God had given me. I should have faced our marital issues with faithfulness and confidence that God would help us overcome them. I should have reacted more positively, and I should have trusted in God's timing. All of these responses would have helped our situation more than what I chose to do. Instead, my faith was paralyzed as I became overwhelmed with disappointment and shame for the lack of our sexual intimacy. I assumed our problems were all my fault, but at the same time, my pride pushed me to find fault in my husband, stirring tension in other areas of our relationship.

>> —————— *Behind the Veil* ——————→

1. The first few weeks of marriage were challenging for us as
    we encountered some of each other's idiosyncrasies and the
    normal need to adjust or compromise when two become
    one. In addition to small differences that we needed to work
    out, our unmet expectations in the bedroom began wearing
    on both of us, affecting our self-control and willingness to
    cooperate in those other areas, such as when one person
    needed a fan to fall asleep while the other needed silence.
    Revisit those first few weeks after you got married. What
    were some difficulties you faced that required compromise?
    What were some expectations you had that were not met?
    How have those unmet expectations affected you?

2. Feeling at fault for our lack of sexual intimacy was a lie I
    adopted and suffered with for a long time. It added to the
    list of obscure and irrational thoughts I had about myself. I
    fought an internal emotional battle I encountered every day,
    which then affected the way I responded to my husband. In
    what ways have you accepted lies about yourself? How have
    those lies affected the way you interact with your husband?

3. Initiating and cultivating romance is not always an easy task,
    especially for someone struggling with insecurity. I chose to
    avoid my husband, fearful of the pain I might encounter. In
    what ways do you struggle with insecurity? How does this
    affect your decision to initiate or cultivate romance?

CHAPTER 10
Change of Scenery

❧

Four weeks after saying "I do," my husband and I were off
on another adventure. We arrived in Washington State late
one February evening. The drive from our hometown in
Southern California had taken almost two days, and Aaron had
been driving for eighteen hours straight, eager to get us to our new
home. We had taken the scenic route on the I-15 north, making
stops in Las Vegas, Idaho, and Montana. The entire drive up, I
couldn't wait to finally reach the state line so I could jump out and
snap a picture in front of the "Welcome to Washington" sign, then
upload it to my then-choice social network MySpace to inform
everyone that we had made it safely.

The fact that we barely got to the state line before the sky
turned completely dark caused some anxiety, but what frustrated
me even more was that the sign stood directly between us and
oncoming traffic.

*Who puts a welcome sign where it can't be reached by the enthu-
siastic travelers who want to take a picture in front of it?* I thought.

Aaron found it amusing, laughing at my fury. Despite not taking a photo in front of the welcome sign, I was relieved that we
had arrived.

Several hours later, we pulled up to our new apartment on the main street in the small town of Lynden. It sat above a print shop next to one other apartment. We were newlyweds, living on a tight budget as we had moved to Washington to begin raising support for a short-term missions assignment we hoped to take. Instead of the normal couch and coffee table for our living room, we settled for a contemporary blue plastic love seat, chair, and footstool—all inflatable! We spent about three hours with the furniture donors, our friends Mike and Tricia, trying to blow these decorative pieces to full capacity, wasting most of our breath laughing at our situation. The furniture remained in decent condition only for about a week, maybe two, before they began to deflate. After that, we couldn't fully inflate them. For the majority of our stay in Washington, we were left with just a backstop of a deflated love seat, which we spent a lot of our free time leaning against in front of the television.

There were a few other small situations I was not prepared for as a new wife. One day as I prepared to open a can of tuna for lunch, it dawned on me that we did not own a can opener. Apparently there are a ton of small things needed to run a home efficiently, tools and skills I was definitely going to need to pick up fast. I ran down the street to a resale shop and purchased a can opener, cheese grater, strainer, and curling iron, all for less than three dollars! That would not be my only trip to the local thrift store.

As much as I desired to be a resourceful wife, I was pathetic in the kitchen. The extent of my cooking knowledge was summed up in cereal, sandwiches, salt, and pepper. I remember on one occasion, while Aaron was at work, I decided to cook a spaghetti dinner. Since I was new in the kitchen, having no clue how to cook, I called home to get a few tips from my mom. Apparently spaghetti making is a commonsense sort of art, a simple dish that should be in every wife's arsenal. That night I served the perfect pot of spaghetti, which my husband loved. My phone call home, however, became a widespread joke in my family, leaving me feeling all the more inadequate.

I might not have been a master chef, but Aaron didn't seem to mind. And I found other things that were easy to enjoy and appreciate about being a wife. We were best friends living in a new place where opportunities to explore were abundant. We visited nearby towns, beaches, and border crossings into Canada. We witnessed the interactions of bald eagles, experienced a few snowfalls, and got lost driving through miles of farmland. We spent time walking through beautiful neighborhoods, talking about the struggles we were facing or what God was teaching us. Our life together was thrilling and, most of the time, incredibly fun.

Almost so thrilling that it eclipsed our bedroom issues.

⊛　⊛　⊛

Aaron and I had hoped that our move to Washington, where we would be on our own and away from anything that could distract us from each other, would ultimately bring us closer together. By changing our environment, we thought we might also set the stage for a positive sexual experience.

This is it, I thought. *This is what we need to enjoy great sex!*

So one night while Aaron was busy at work, I decided to try something that was sure to surprise him. Sifting through my drawers I found a piece of lingerie I knew he had never seen on me. I put it on and then curled my hair and put on makeup. I wanted to exude sexiness, something I rarely ever felt. When I heard the doorknob turn, my heart sank. I was anxious to see how my husband would respond to my makeover, and apprehensive about attempting to initiate sex.

My romantic gesture led us into an evening of togetherness. However, no amount of stimulation or foreplay helped us. Our efforts were relentless, yet our results proved disastrous. A tear rolled down my cheek, sliding past Aaron's nose. He held me tightly.

"Please don't cry," he whispered in my ear.

But I couldn't control it. I had spent all day thinking about how perfect this moment would be, yet we were held back from finding pleasure in one of God's greatest gifts. Because of me.

I could not compose myself, distraught by the pain of intercourse. I felt guilty, as if it were something I could control. But
I tried, and I couldn't. Our romantic night ended with manual
stimulation, which I felt was a cheap form of satisfaction since we
could not experience the real thing. I'm sure we both figured it
would have to hold us over for the time being.

Each night the thought of sex churned in my head. I began
to dread it. As soon as Aaron would make an advance, an excuse
to get to bed early would shoot out of my mouth. I used all the
common ones: headache, fatigue, upset stomach, and the list went
on. I knew it was wrong to deny him so often, but I talked myself
into blaming him most of the time. I would tell him, "You need
to be more sensitive to me and not ask for sex all the time." After
only weeks of being married and sharing the same bed, we began
to fight as if we were enemies.

❀   ❀   ❀

One day Aaron came with me to a health clinic. I'd finally found
the courage to seek some medical advice about our sex situation.
From my flushed skin tone and stuttered words, the nurse could
tell that I wasn't too comfortable talking about it, so she offered
to take a walk with us. That was not the typical response I was
familiar with from a health clinic worker, but we now lived in a
smaller town, where people seemed to take the time to genuinely
care for others. I appreciated her willingness to chat, but it didn't
ease my heart having to explain our situation. As we walked a few
blocks, her willingness to listen helped me share about our sexual
issues. She asked us intentional questions about our interactions
and then advised us to set the mood more romantically by sharing
a bottle of wine, lighting a few candles, and relaxing as much as
possible before proceeding. She even suggested that we have an
intimate night during which we would purposefully abstain from
sex in order to alleviate my anxieties.

I thanked her for spending time with me and left with a small to-do list. Unfortunately, we made no progress; there was no breakthrough, no miracle. I was young, inexperienced, and sexually challenged. I began to regret getting married, but I quickly fought against those thoughts in fear of ever getting close to . . . divorce. I'd experienced divorce's pain firsthand as a child, and I was not about to ever let that become an option!

One night after that Aaron initiated intimacy. I wanted to enjoy sex! But again we spent more than an hour "trying." In the middle of Aaron exploring the curves of my body, the burden became too great and my spirit broke. Tears flowed like a river.

He stopped and kindly told me that we didn't have to keep going. "Let's go watch a movie and get our minds off of this." Any sort of distraction to dismiss the pain.

As much as I appreciated his willingness to change things up, I was furious that we couldn't have sex. I felt cheated, robbed of romance. Night after night my husband would show his love for me, passionately pursuing me and desiring just a moment of intimacy with me. And night after night I simply couldn't push through the pain.

Sometimes a sharp pang of emotion burst out from within and I would scream into my pillow to mask the piercing sound of my heart's cry. Sometimes I couldn't even muster the energy to cry and instead simply stared blankly, drowning in hopelessness. Snapping out of self-pity was a challenge for me and a chore for my husband. We regularly tried to find ways to take our minds off our struggle. Although the ache fled for short periods, the longing to have a fulfilled marriage weighed heavy on me.

❈   ❈   ❈

As we settled into our new home, we were able to build friendships with a few families. Yet no matter how close we became to other couples, I never felt comfortable enough to reach out to anyone regarding our sex issue, except for the kind nurse. And honestly, I wasn't ready to address it myself. I was trapped, listening to the lies

I told myself: *I'm the only one struggling like this. It's too embarrassing to talk about. No one will understand.*

One dark, cold night as Aaron and I cuddled on the bed, we began to kiss and touch each other. While wrapped tightly in each other's arms, we prayed aloud that God would make this night different from the rest. Yes, we prayed aloud during sex! We so desired to be fulfilled in this area of our marriage that we literally cried out to God for help. We prayed for healing, restoration, and breakthrough.

Joy filled our hearts as hope rose from our faith. We continued to engage, enveloped in each other's warmth. Then the moment of attempting the physical act of oneness came. It did not matter how slow we went, the pain intensified. Aaron must have felt my body tense and he backed away from me. It was so excruciating I couldn't help but cry.

I was irate that we had prayed and God had done nothing to intervene. I ran to the bathroom sobbing. I locked the bathroom door, turned on the shower, and dropped to my knees. Clutching my chest, I tried to relieve the anxiety I felt suffocating me. I beat my thighs with clenched fists to redirect the pain throbbing in my lower region, as well as the emotional pain aching in my heart. The water ran over me like a waterfall, flushing the tears from my eyes. Through screams and cries I told God how angry I was, begging Him to intercede and help us. I pleaded with Him to cleanse me, to heal me, and to fix me. I was ashamed that the idea of sex was a burden to me. I felt guilty for not being available to my husband, and I struggled with feeling as if I were in some way broken.

My husband knocked louder and louder as he tried desperately to get in. I could hear his compassion, worry, and exhaustion in the way he said my name.

In that moment I thought, *How could a marriage between two strong believers come to this so quickly?*

We felt weakened, stripped down, and beaten over the very thing that God purposed us for in marriage—an intimate relationship.

I opened the door, falling into my husband's arms. With the water still running, Aaron moved me back to the shower and we slid our backs against the wall with our knees to our chests. I laid my head on his shoulder. We sat in silence beneath the water, beneath the heaviness that weighed over our relationship.

It took every last bit of strength to climb back into bed. My husband wanted to talk about all I was feeling, but all I could whisper back was, "Indescribable." It was difficult to fall asleep that night.

I felt as though I was living a lie. On the surface, I'm sure we seemed like a mature Christian couple with a beautiful life, but the truth is that I was silently suffering. Our hearts were torn in different directions as we passionately wanted to serve the God we love, all while bitterness and anger were driving roots deeper into our souls. The ideal of a perfect marriage seemed just as unwelcoming and unattainable as the Washington state line sign.

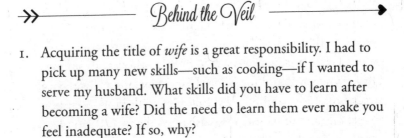

Behind the Veil

1. Acquiring the title of *wife* is a great responsibility. I had to pick up many new skills—such as cooking—if I wanted to serve my husband. What skills did you have to learn after becoming a wife? Did the need to learn them ever make you feel inadequate? If so, why?

2. As we are growing up, we generally aren't taught how to be sexual in a healthy way. Unfortunately, most of our exposure as to what sexiness means is perverted through marketing and moneymaking businesses that culture has deemed acceptable. Feeling sexy, however, is important in marriage as it encourages a positive attitude/posture toward sex. Have you ever struggled to view yourself as sexy? In what ways have you tried to feel that way for your husband? In those

times, did it help you and your husband come together for a better experience?

3. I would not understand the effects of my rejection of sex or its importance to my husband until years later. My rejection compounded over time, damaging our relationship and hurting my husband deeply. Do you reject your husband when he pursues physical intimacy with you? If so, what excuses do you use and what motivates you to avoid sex?

CHAPTER 11

A Trip to Africa

As the plane descended onto the asphalt runway, my immediate impression was that the landscape screamed "Africa!" The contrast of green treetops and red dirt was vibrant against the bright blue sky. I was flooded with a mixture of different feelings: I was excited finally to be in Africa, ready to serve God as He had prepared us to, but I was also nervous about what Aaron and I would face in a developing country. All I could do was take one step at a time, and getting off the plane was my first goal.

Aaron and I had decided to go to Africa just before our wedding, and by God's grace, we raised nearly fourteen thousand dollars during our three months in Washington—enough to cover all our costs. Along with the pressure of becoming a wife, and amid our marital struggles, I had been preparing to travel to the other side of the world to fulfill my dream of doing mission work with my husband. Four months into marriage, we had said good-bye to our friends in Lynden and left the life we knew in the States to join new friends in Zambia, the same mission destination Aaron had traveled to just before he proposed to me almost a year earlier.

After we made our way through customs and met members of the organization we would be working with, thirteen of us piled into a large truck, which took us through downtown Livingstone

before veering onto a dirt path. As I soaked in all the new scenery
and unfamiliar scents, I glanced over at my husband. He looked
peaceful. All of this was familiar to him, and I could tell he was
excited to be back.

The truck continued to bounce and wobble down the road.
On either side of us rose tall grass, surpassing the height of an aver-
age man. The sun was sitting just above the horizon, and every few
seconds it would shine through the slender green and yellow stalks.
For a moment everything seemed to happen in slow motion—the
colors were brilliant and the lighting was perfect; it felt like a pic-
turesque clip from a movie. The truck began to slow and the sound
of children's voices singing broke the surreal movie scene. I glanced
over the edge of the truck frame and saw kids running beside us,
wearing the most joyous smiles I had ever seen.

It was dark by the time we reached our base. We had just
enough energy to eat dinner and crash; the full tour of the property would have to wait until the next day. We received our sleeping arrangements, and I knew immediately we were in for a treat.
The idea of a nice, cozy house or even an apartment fashioned to
my liking was far from my mind. In fact, our small, two-person
tent was just as fascinating as a dog igloo, with no room to deco-
rate and less insulation. Our new living quarters barely fit our two
bodies, let alone our baggage, which sat just outside our tent.

After we'd spent two nights trying to adjust to our lodging, an
army of ants that refused to retreat assaulted us, so we begged for
reassignment. We moved into a same-sized tent, free from ants.
It was supposed to be a temporary settlement until a much bigger tent was constructed. However, that 6' x 6' tent served as our
space for the next two months. It was not an ideal newlywed pad,
but we managed.

The nights were ice cold. We had heard that sleeping naked in
our sleeping bags would keep us warmer than layering on night
clothes. For several weeks we shivered through the nights in our
bare skin. When we finally realized that our sleeping bags were

not as high quality as we'd thought they were, we joked about how lucky we were that we hadn't frozen to death . . . naked. Then we started layering on our clothes at night, and often we zipped our sleeping bags together. Those nights, when we cuddled together for warmth, will always be one of my favorite newlywed experiences. My husband would likely disagree, as I tend to kick and twirl throughout the night.

The main building of our ministry organization's base sat close to the edge of a gorge: a mile-long, vertical drop where the Zambezi River flows east of Victoria Falls. The opposite side of the ravine looked like an endless plateau of African desert. Most nights we gathered at the edge of the gorge to witness a majestic sunset, colors flaming across the giant horizon, that was followed by a thick darkness falling across the sky, reminding us that we were out in the middle of nowhere.

We often had a campfire that shone like a candle in a big, dark room. Everyone's faces reflected warmth and light, radiating obvious passion to reveal the gospel to those whom we'd traveled far to meet. Around that campfire we shared stories of our pasts to get to know each of the missionaries we were serving with, we retold testimonies of God's power, we read Scripture aloud, and we worshiped God together. Every morning we rose with the sun and gathered back around the fire pit for prayer. By then the fire was nothing more than a few embers with a single line of smoldering smoke, but we knew we would enjoy another fire that night. The miraculous stories told around that pit bolstered my faith; I counted on our camaraderie and the stories of God's victory to strengthen us as a team.

⊛ ⊛ ⊛

One morning Aaron and I woke up with a desire for each other. It had been weeks since we had attempted to have sex. Based on our track record with sexual intimacy, it was easiest and most comfortable to allow ourselves to be distracted by our lives in Africa.

Although having sex was still difficult, we were not ready to give up trying.

We took extra precaution to make sure we were super quiet, since we knew the tents were horrible insulators of warmth and sound. Although again we were not successful at having sex, we did enjoy each other.

Shortly afterward we got ready for the day and headed to breakfast, where about twenty other missionaries joined us. My mind was focused on getting oatmeal when the biggest guy in the place smiled and made a sarcastic remark about not walking by "the Smiths' tent in the morning!" I don't know if he was joking or had heard us earlier that morning, but my face turned red. For an instant I regretted our choice to come to Africa, as well as our decision to pursue sex.

I felt frustrated and started to wallow in self-pity. Not only were we living without privacy, we were constantly in danger of getting sick or attacked by some wild animal or insect. Meanwhile *nearly every other newly married couple* began their lives together by building a home and getting good jobs, which then led to extending their families and their finances. With those thoughts, I tucked another piece of ammo into the pocket of my heart that I could use against my husband whenever I felt like our life was not up to par. In my frustrations, I would always find a way to justify my feelings while blaming him. And I know I hurt him often.

Usually in my moments of weakness, Aaron would throw his arms around me and hold me tightly. His embrace was familiar and his presence calmed me, and I would remember again *why* we had chosen this life. Our Creator had called us to invest in His Kingdom. While most couples spend the majority of their days working independently, my husband and I were working together. Although most spouses learn about each other's character traits through different situations that come randomly throughout the years, we were confronted with these differences daily. We were living outside our comfort zone; we were threatened by unfamiliar diseases; we were challenged in our faith when fearful situations arose, such as being hustled by money changers on the street; and we were forced to rely on God's provision of food and drinking water. We needed each other's support every single day or else we would have crumbled under the pressure of our circumstances. Every time I began to doubt or question why I was there, God spoke to me gently through the arms of my husband, reminding me why I was serving Him in Africa alongside my best friend.

⊛　⊛　⊛

We learned a great deal about each other in the four months we spent in Africa. It was as if God was helping us to know each other on a deeper level, using our circumstances to peel back another layer of our hearts. Although the process was slow, God was showing me just how much trust plays a role in being able to be unveiled. Aaron observed how I can be controlled by my fears, how I show my compassion to serve others, how I easily break down emotionally, how I question theology in an effort to gain understanding, and how I lack zeal for foreign foods. I discovered Aaron's thrill for adventure, I learned from his knowledge of God, I saw him encourage others, I watched him sacrifice things to bless others, I saw his confidence in the face of threats, and I was profoundly inspired as I experienced his love for me in extraordinary ways, such as when he learned a song on the guitar in only one week so he could surprise me with it, just because he knew I thought it would be romantic. We laughed together, we cried together, and we shared all the emotions in between.

We made lifelong friendships with other couples, we stood at the edge of Victoria Falls, and we white-water rafted down the Zambezi, which was filled with alligators. We hiked dirt trails and cliff sides, we ate exotic food, and sometimes we didn't get to eat at all. We got lost way too many times, we sat beneath some of the most amazing stars, we sang alongside beautiful Africans who had more joy than we had ever witnessed, and we danced because they danced. We learned how to cook over an open fire, we went to the bathroom surrounded by bushes, we ran out of money often, and we encountered God in a way that we'd never needed to before.

I will forever be grateful for the opportunity to spread God's love in a foreign land. I believe it impacted my heart and my character in profound ways. The adventures I faced in Africa challenged me to think outside the American culture I was familiar with. I realized I'd have to trade life as I had always known it for a completely different lifestyle if I was going to follow after God. His ways are simply not our ways.

My adventure in Africa was an incredible blessing as I encountered moments that simply took my breath away, such as when I played with the sweet young children and witnessed miracles by God's powerful hand. Yet there were also trying moments, including a two-month battle with a yeast infection and my extreme anxiety about catching a deadly disease. It can be challenging to retell an adventure that so often seemed to move back and forth from good to bad experiences. Marriage is often experienced the same way: an ebb and flow of good times and more difficult ones.

Among the many high and low points throughout our time in Africa, there was one constant: a strain bearing down on our marriage because of separation anxiety. I grew up feeling close to my family and dependent on them. The distance between us became a threat, a flaming arrow toward my marriage. Almost every day, I told Aaron how much I missed my family. I felt discontentment at being so far from them and wondering what I was missing back home, which translated into harsh actions toward my husband. I often mentioned my desire to head home or how excited I would be when our time in Africa came to an end. My husband responded by sharing how he hoped I would be able to find joy no matter where God was leading us. Although I understood Aaron's point of view and unending encouragement, I found it difficult to accept, and my separation anxiety worsened.

The challenges I faced in Africa seemed to amplify whenever

I had no way to communicate with my mother. I knew being married meant that I was supposed to cling to my husband, but I became obsessive about needing to be back home. I justified my feelings by telling myself I was not ready to be a missionary in a foreign land, nor was I ready to chart the waters of marriage. Being away from home convinced me that I was ill equipped to be a wife—another unmet expectation to add to my growing list.

Behind the Veil

1. I didn't have too many expectations of our time in Africa. However, I did have one huge misconception: I thought I would give more of myself in Africa than I would gain. Instead, I learned so much about the culture and was blessed way beyond what I tried to contribute while there. Have you and your husband encountered something life changing together? In what ways did you grow closer together or further apart during that experience?

2. Facing hardships together drew things out of my and my husband's characters that helped us get to know each other better. In what ways have hardships or trials helped you get to know your husband? What are some of those things you learned about him?

3. Amid our sexual challenges and my doubts about our decision to marry, God never stopped pursuing an intimate relationship with me. Between my fits of discontent and anxiety in Africa, I encountered God's love in a beautiful way, even if it was just time I spent in prayer overlooking the gorge. I felt Him near. During the hardships or doubts you may have encountered early in your marriage, did you acknowledge God or were you too distracted by pain to spend time with Him?

CHAPTER 12
Embittered by Jealousy

❧

Darkness surrounded me in our tent. I could hear voices in the distance, people walking back and forth across the base. I yearned to be included in the laughter and joy of spending time with everyone else who had traveled to Zambia as missionaries, but it was a challenge for me, especially on these nights. My introverted personality often hindered me like this, and I was trapped by a looming fear that I didn't know how to fit in with others. The worry of having to figure out what to say or what to do clouded my mind. I convinced myself that staying inside was the safest choice, yet I didn't realize how quickly my negative thoughts would spiral out of control. I felt isolated and alone, burning with frustrations that didn't make sense. All notions of logic had disappeared and I was running off emotional fumes.

Adjusting to the culture and climate of Africa seemed slightly less difficult than the adjustment to marriage. Six months had already passed since our wedding, and I was still searching to gain my bearings as a wife. And tonight, two months into our time in Africa, rocking back and forth in my tent, I could not believe the intensity of my emotions. My heart thumped loudly as my mind swirled with irrational thoughts, agitated by something I never knew I struggled with: jealousy.

My oblivious husband was working late into the night on a project for the mission organization. Aaron and I had two different service missions in Africa: he handled web development, graphic design, and social media, while I studied theology, wilderness response, and cultural diversity; handled service projects for the base; and got to know the villagers alongside my teammates. Although we were blessed with opportunities to share the gospel side by side, our responsibilities often kept us busy and apart. Aaron found a niche in the office next to a friend, where they spent hours creating and redesigning things like the website and other promotional materials.

I was learning that my husband's passion to help others required much of his time and energy. Although I knew that he was doing good things, no amount of reassurance could stop the waves of insecurity from crashing over me. Once I bent beneath their pressure, I became weak to the "dark side" of jealousy.

Thought after thought attacked me as I lay in my little tent. I was jealous that Aaron had the opportunity to work on creative projects with the staff, and I was envious of any time he spent with anyone other than me. My anger built as I interpreted my husband's actions through the skewed lens of jealousy, believing he didn't care about me or that he didn't want to spend time with me. I figured if he thought about me at all, he would have checked in to see what I was up to. Hours had passed that day since I had last seen him.

He must not care, I thought.

My protectiveness over our marriage became a raging obsession, distracting me from spending time with God, other friends, and even my husband. I suppose I could have gone to check in on him, but in my frustration I waited for him to come to me. I had anticipated that he would want to spend time with his wife rather than working late—again. I created scenarios of the most perfect and romantic ways he would call for me or come to see me. When those didn't happen and I remained alone in a small, dark tent, anger and bitterness grew.

I began to believe the worst about my husband. My jealousy quickly led to doubts about our love.

He probably doesn't like being married, I thought. *He wants to leave me. He is resentful because of the trials we've faced.*

I had no proof that what I believed of my husband was true. I was fabricating it, sewing each thought together with the thread of insecurity. And it all happened so fast.

❁   ❁   ❁

When I heard my husband finally approach our tent, I laid my head down and closed my eyes, pretending to be asleep. All I desired was for him to wrap me in his arms and pour out his love for me, yet he remained quiet. Sliding into bed next to me, he laid his head inches from mine. Only three sounds could I hear in that moment: the random howls of nocturnal creatures, the peaceful whisper of my husband's sleepy sigh, and anger screaming from within me. I wanted nothing more than to burst at the seams, but I remained silent, hoping my husband would rescue me from myself.

After hours of sulking and stewing that night, I broke down and told Aaron how I was feeling. He tried to communicate his intentions behind his decisions, telling me he had slipped into bed because he did not want to wake his sleeping beauty. He was completely unaware of my pain, and he encouraged me to vocalize my issues *before* they got out of control. He wanted the opportunity to fix any problems he caused, but he couldn't if I didn't explain how his behavior hurt me. I tried to share with him how upset I was and how it seemed he lacked a desire to spend time with me, but expressing such vulnerability made me uncomfortable.

Communicating how I felt was terribly hard to do. In addition to having to find the right words, I became embarrassed as I realized how irrational I was being. There was no way I could tell my husband all of that, especially if I still wanted my feelings to matter to him and for him to want to spend time with me.

>> ———————— *Behind the Veil* ————————➤

1. This episode with jealousy would not be my last. Countless times since then I have been wrought with jealousy over my husband's opportunities, his wisdom, the time he's spent away from me, the people he interacts with, and more recently, his role as a father. In what ways do you get jealous over your husband?

2. Before I was married, I never would have seen that jealousy could become a sin I would have to combat. Although I sometimes struggled with it while dating, I thought the security of marriage would suppress any motivation for jealousy. After I became a wife, though, the intensity of my emotions helped me see my jealousy more clearly, an imperfection I would rather not admit to having. Sometimes I would sit alone in our tent (or in our car or in our bedroom, during different seasons of our marriage), and spin my wheels thinking about Aaron not loving me or wanting to leave me—things he had never provided any proof of. Do you struggle with jealousy toward your husband? If so, what are some reasons you get jealous? How does being jealous affect your marriage?

3. Allowing jealousy to run amok in my heart happened even on those really good days, when my husband was romantic and *did* show me how much he valued our marriage. For some reason, it didn't matter if he did ten or twenty cherishing things for me; if he took one step outside of my expectations, my hurt was enough to make me doubt his love. Have you noticed that jealousy has no boundaries, and the more you feed it, the more irrational your thoughts are toward your husband? Why is this dangerous for your marriage relationship?

4. Aaron would often confront me during these episodes, and we would end up fighting. Although I fought to defend the validation I thought I deserved, inside I was embarrassed. I had no way to discern why I felt the way I did. As a newlywed, I feared that Aaron would think, *Who did I marry?*—a question even I felt I could never answer for him. My insecurities piled on top of one another, pressuring me to falter as a wife. Although it was a challenge for me to express how I was feeling toward Aaron, the bold confrontation that night in our tent helped me face reality directly, another part of the process of being unveiled. In moments when jealousy runs wild, do you fight to justify your point of view or try to defend your desire for your husband to validate your feelings? How does jealousy increase the power of insecurity?

CHAPTER 13

Is Marriage a Mistake?

A aron and I sat at the end of a small wooden dock that stretched out past the mild wake of Lake Malawi in Africa. We had been staying in Cape Maclear for several days sharing the gospel and encouraging some of the teachers in town. We knew we would be leaving this piece of paradise landscape nestled on the shoreline in less than an hour to make our trek back to our base in Livingstone and then home to see our families, so Aaron and I took our window of opportunity to soak up as much of its beauty as possible.

We sat beneath a simply-built gazebo that shaded us from the bright noon sun. With our legs dangling inches from the surface of the crystal clear water, we noticed the exotic tropical fish swimming everywhere. It is remarkable how a new experience in a beautiful place can be a catalyst for deep conversation. We were just as transparent with each other as the water was beneath us, revealing struggles we were facing individually and the issues we were experiencing in our marriage. We connected in such a special way in that moment that it felt as if the whole world stopped spinning, except for the abundance of tropical fish dancing beneath us in the crystal-blue water. We both took a deep breath to relax. We reaffirmed our love for each other with uplifting words. I told Aaron that I still had faith that we would survive the intimacy crisis we were having,

75

hoping that it would get better as our marriage grew. Aaron assured me that he would continue to be patient, and I told him I would try to find a solution to help us. We were determined to experience a fulfilled marriage, willing to wait unwaveringly until that day would come. We walked back toward town, with Aaron's arm wrapped around my waist and joy consuming my heart.

Less than an hour later, after praying with the other missionaries, we tied our luggage to the top of our seven-passenger truck, said good-bye to our host family, and headed for our base camp 860 miles away. Aaron and I had spent a month in Malawi with three other missionaries and two translators. It had been a rugged reconnaissance, testing our faith the times we were stranded in a desolate place or when food was scarce, while also providing opportunities to share with others how true our God is. But the brief rest and relaxation we had encountered on the dock earlier that morning seemed to give me a boost of strength.

⊛　⊛　⊛

Aaron was driving a group of us down a deeply rutted dirt path. We were less than forty miles into our trip when all of a sudden the truck felt as though it were being lifted off the road as we drifted at an angle.

Everything seemed to happen in slow motion. We were all silent, except for a scared voice screaming from the backseat, "Jesus, Jesus, Jesus, please Jesus, please!"

I looked out the windshield and made eye contact with an old man riding a bicycle. He must have been in his sixties and was wearing a fisherman's hat that made him resemble Gilligan from the TV show *Gilligan's Island*. His face mirrored the fear that I knew was obvious on mine. We were headed directly toward him until the frame of the car blocked my view. Aaron's counter steer sent us sliding in a different direction.

Within a second, the giant metal beast collided with the earth, rolling with force and then stopping on its side. I'm not sure if I closed my eyes for half a blink or blacked out—time seemed to blur. As my friend above me crawled out of the top through a passenger window, I looked down to see what I could stand on, knowing that my other friend lay beneath me.

Is she alive? I wondered, since all I could see was her limp body up to her shoulder. I knew my weight was bearing down on her so I quickly crawled out of the wreck.

As soon as my feet hit the dirt, I heard my husband's voice, "Are you okay, baby?"

"I think so. My hair feels wet. Am I bleeding?"

"No, you're not bleeding." Gripping me tightly in his arms, he kept repeating, "I'm so sorry!"

As he guided me off to the side of the road, I glanced back to see my friend climb out of the truck.

"She's alive!" I whispered.

Malawians came running down the street and out of the forest, immediately helping us. Men worked together to flip the truck back on its wheels, while women and children huddled around our belongings, some of which we had pulled from the truck and some that had flown out onto the road. Malawi is known as "the warm heart of Africa" because of the reputation of its people. We experienced their warm hearts that day and were truly grateful for their aid.

The men rolled the truck back down the road to a small market where they spent forty-five minutes pushing the roof out by kicking it and welding some of the pieces back to its frame. Everyone got back inside the truck, ready to get to our final destination— everyone but me. I stood on the road looking at the mess of a truck, in shock over what we had endured. I didn't want to get back inside. I didn't trust it anymore. Most of the windows were busted out, including the windshield, and the doors barely shut. I was reluctant to get in the vehicle, but I knew I did not have another option.

From the point of getting into that truck, my only desire was to go home, back to my family. I wanted familiarity. I wanted comfort. The accident wiped me out, and I used the only energy I had left wishing to be home.

Over the course of a week, we spent three and a half hours in our truck, more than eighteen hours on a bus, about two hours on taxi services, sixteen hours on a one-stop flight back to the States, and seemingly countless miles on foot carrying our belongings on our backs, not to mention the late nights we spent trying to navigate our way through transportation stations and hostels. Simply put, I was exhausted physically, emotionally, and mentally.

❁   ❁   ❁

After four and a half months our ministry time in Africa was done, but before we could be welcomed home, we had one more mission assignment scheduled: El Salvador. When preparing for Africa, we had planned to attend a conference for missionaries in Central America, a short detour that would last only seven days. Our flight from Zambia was long and touched down in Miami, behind schedule. We rushed from our gate to another departure gate on the other side of the airport terminal to catch our connecting flight to La Libertad, El Salvador.

With only minutes to board the plane, Aaron and I, along with a handful of missionaries, ran through the airport. We were about halfway to our gate when exhaustion overwhelmed me. I had not slept well since the accident, especially on the long flight we had just finished. During the sixteen-hour plane ride, we had encountered bouts of turbulence that made me cringe in fear, and I hoped we would not face another accident. In the middle of the bustling airport, I gave up. I stopped running. My bottom lip began to quiver, and standing still in a sea of travelers, I began to cry. Aaron must have noticed my absence quickly, because in a flash he returned to my side.

"What's the matter, baby?"

"I can't do it! I just want to go home. I think you married the wrong girl!"

Aaron grabbed my hand and said firmly, "C'mon, we'll talk about it on the plane."

We didn't have time to waste on my doubt, and my husband's tone helped me snap back into reality. I held on to his hand as we ran to make our flight. Out of breath and flushed with pink faces, we handed the gatekeeper our tickets to scan, the last of the passengers to board the flight. Once we sat down and buckled in for the flight, Aaron held his hand up to my warm cheek, reminded me that we would be in El Salvador for only seven days, assured me that I could make it, and then in the sweetest voice said, "I definitely married the right girl." He kissed my forehead and encouraged me to try to get some rest.

I knew my dramatic outburst in the airport was the result of being extremely worn out. But struggling with the thought that I had made a mistake getting married was a growing doubt that had been oppressing me on and off for months. My heart was in the trenches of a perilous battle.

El Salvador was a lovely place, and the conference we attended was inspiring to my faith. However, in the midst of our adventure, I experienced inner turmoil. Not only did I wonder if my marriage was a mistake, now I was conflicted with thoughts of reconciling that doubt with thoughts of perhaps becoming a single woman again. I fought every day to keep those thoughts suppressed, convicted to the core that I could not go down the devastating road of divorce.

As we finally returned home to California, I knew we would need to keep chasing distractions or the pain of our failing marriage would catch up to us and ultimately erode the love that had motivated us to say "I do."

>> ———— *Behind the Veil* ————>

1. Aaron and I literally went from experiencing the most peace we'd ever felt in our relationship to feeling as if our lives

had been threatened. The truck accident reminded me that the enemy is very real and hates to see marriages thrive, especially when the husband and wife are passionate about serving God. In what ways do you recognize how the enemy has come against your marriage or your lives?

2. The events that took place during our trip to Africa influenced my outlook on life and my relationship with my husband. By the end of our four months there, I was thankful for all we had endured, but I also felt ready to return to the comfort and familiarity of home. What events occurred shortly after your marriage that either brought you and your husband closer together or threatened your relationship? What was your response to those events? Did you find security in God and your husband, or did you hope for security in your family?

3. Every challenging situation in our marriage made me feel insecure. Every time I was pushed out of my comfort zone, I scrutinized our relationship. Doubt filled my mind with all kinds of reasons why we never should have gotten married. Stopping in the airport that afternoon was a breaking point due to the stress. I believe it was crucial for me to address that growing doubt, a part of my unveiling that would let my husband know me a little deeper. However, that moment in the airport did not provide an atmosphere in which to safely talk through and reconcile how I was feeling. Unfortunately, my emotions tossed me back and forth for years, as I quietly wondered if my marriage was a mistake. Have you ever struggled with thoughts like this? If so, what were some triggers that motivated you to doubt the love between you and your husband?

CHAPTER 14

I'm Broken

❧

After slipping into the sheer paper robe, I waited quietly for the gynecologist to enter the room. Memories of my wedding flooded my mind. It was hard to believe a year had passed since Aaron and I had said our vows. We had done so much as newlyweds, but celebrating was difficult for us, as we still had not successfully consummated our marriage. I resisted this appointment for a while, afraid of feeling physically uncomfortable and of the possibility that something more serious was wrong with my body. Yet I had promised Aaron on the wooden dock in Malawi that I would search for help, and this was one of my first attempts.

A hard knock announced the doctor's arrival. My anxiety spiked. The big white door swung open as she walked in, looked at a clipboard, and began to ask me questions.

"I see here that you're married. How long have you been married?"

"We just celebrated our one-year anniversary," I replied.

"Congratulations!" She smiled. "So are you on any birth control?"

"No." I had stopped taking birth control two months after we were married. I thought it was lowering my libido, and since we weren't really having sex, I decided it was unnecessary.

"Oh, you guys are trying to conceive?"

"No, we're not."

"Okay, do you want me to prescribe some birth control?"

"No, thank you. I am actually here because my husband and I are not able to have sex, and I was wondering if you could help," I explained sheepishly.

She looked baffled. "Why do you think you can't have sex?"

"Every time we try, it causes extreme pain down there."

"What kind of pain?"

"Burning or tearing sensations."

"Well, let's take a look and see what's going on." After a few minutes of assessment, the doctor exclaimed enthusiastically, "Everything checks out great! You are young and healthy, and there should be nothing keeping you from having great sex."

Grief swelled up in my heart like helium filling a balloon. I gulped my sadness as I tried to describe a little more of my inability to have sex, but the doctor's final piece of advice included the same old recipe of setting the mood better.

Most people would be thrilled to receive such a positive report, yet I was wallowing in self-pity because, according to her, nothing was wrong with me. Aaron was just as disappointed when I gave him the news. I felt that at least if we knew what was wrong, even if it was serious, we could fix it. Despite my longing, I was still without a cure.

Not only had we not gained any understanding from a medical professional, the doctor had also reinforced the idea that I was alone in my struggle. Regardless of the good news the doctor had shared with me, I couldn't stop repeating these words: *I'm so broken.*

I was confused and angry. I begged God for healing, but from my perspective He didn't seem interested. And I believed that Aaron and I were the only married couple who experienced such a strange problem. Assaulted by anxious thoughts, I continued to compare my marriage to other marriages. What we were going through just didn't seem fair. In my fragile state, I thought complaining to God was reasonable, but it left me feeling all the more disconnected from Him. One grievance upon another had me clutching for my veil, wanting nothing more than to keep hiding behind it.

As my fury raged, I yelled out to God, "You told me to save myself for marriage. You told me to serve You. I know You have the power to heal me, so why won't You? I don't want this kind of life! I don't want to be mad at You, but I am. I hate that You won't help us!"

>> ———— *Behind the Veil* ————➤

1. I gathered the courage to seek out an answer for our marital issue, but it resulted in nothing. This only fueled my frustrations and reinforced my feeling of being alone. We were supposed to celebrate our anniversary with joy, but it seemed unreasonable. Were you able to celebrate your one-year wedding anniversary, or were there growing contentions in your marriage by that time? Have you struggled with loneliness since becoming a wife?

2. On the surface Aaron and I were fine: we were best friends, soul mates destined to experience life abundantly. Yet secretly I grew tired of not feeling satisfied. I harbored anger toward God, and I became bitter toward the idea of intimacy. It took everything in me to wake up each morning and continue to persevere. Some days were harder than others. Have you experienced dissatisfaction, anger, or bitterness toward God or your husband because of your marriage? If so, in what ways have these emotions affected these two relationships?

3. As my insecurities led me to question God about fairness in comparison to other marriages, I became angry with

Him. Instead of blossoming into the wife I thought I would be, I felt like marriage was breaking me down more and more. In what ways have you compared your marriage to other marriages? What resulted from these comparisons?

CHAPTER 15

Puffed Up

P acking up our car took us only forty minutes. All of our belongings fit compactly into the backseat and trunk of our Jetta. Although our stuff had a place to rest, my husband and I did not have a place to call our own. We had moved to Florida shortly after our trips to Africa and El Salvador, chasing after our desire to live an extraordinary life and to meet our need for distraction. Now we'd agreed to volunteer in the office of the mission organization we'd served overseas, which seemed like an honorable way to satisfy both of those needs.

Since coming to the Sunshine State, we had already relocated twice, living with families willing to support us with temporary housing. Aaron and I had part-time jobs in addition to volunteering in the office, but we were unable to afford our own place on our limited budget. For six weeks, we were able to house-sit for a family while they were on vacation. But now that they were scheduled to come home, we knew we needed another gift of hospitality. In a town we were just getting to know, we had nowhere to go, except the privacy of our faithful little car.

Sitting anxiously on the edge of my seat, I leaned toward the driver's side to see just how far the gas gauge was falling under the red line. The yellow warning light had been shouting at us for a while. Finally finding a gas station, my husband and I coasted into the lot, simultaneously releasing an exhale of relief. We made it. Or did we?

We'd been trying desperately to establish ourselves here, but it was difficult to get ahead financially and so we'd been living week to week. On the day we pulled into the gas station, we still had two days to wait for our paycheck. And we had no money.

Moving to Florida after wanting nothing more than to be back with my family was a tough decision for me, but Aaron felt sure it would be good for us. I desired to follow my husband, and so I did, trusting he was right. A year and a half had passed since we'd pledged our love to each other in holy matrimony. Every moment of our time together had been as exciting as it had been trying, and we were still just getting started.

My husband sat in the driver's seat and let out a sigh. Then he made a humble call home, asking his mom for a small transfer to help us out with some gas, a loan to carry us over until we got paid.

I waved my hand to grab his attention, shaking my head from side to side, hoping he could read my lips, "Don't tell her we're homeless!"

I wanted our parents to be proud of us and all that we were accomplishing. Though we were passionately striving to be world changers by volunteering for the mission organization, I knew the news of our being homeless would have overshadowed the good.

Fortunately Aaron's mom sent us the money, no questions asked. Brimming with gas in our tank, along with all of our belongings, we prayed God would help us find a place to call home. Praying may have been the righteous thing to do, and I am glad we did; however, it was accompanied by a selfish and prideful attitude fueled by the tensions of our circumstances. *God, is this how You take care of the ones who serve You unselfishly? We aren't asking for a mansion here! Why would my husband bring us across the United States with no way to provide for us? Can I even trust him?* Thought after thought raced through my mind, questioning why we were homeless when we were trying hard to serve God. Besides the bags of clothes and our car, we had nothing to our name.

❀   ❀   ❀

Although we had made the decision together to become missionaries, knowing full well the sacrifices required, I was frustrated and found a way to blame my husband for our hardships. In a time when we needed to support each other the most, I furiously kicked down the foundation of our relationship.

"Are you going to get a better job? If you don't, we aren't going to make it like this! We need a place of our own; otherwise we should just go back home."

"Okay, babe," was all he said.

These types of conversations usually ended in an argument. Aaron would cut off my complaint and remind me that following God is not always comfortable. He would tell me I needed to have joy no matter what our circumstances were. And he would bring up how we came to Florida to volunteer our time and talents, which we would not be able to do with full-time jobs.

All I could fathom was how impossible his idea of living seemed to be, and how our situation proved I was right. Our bickering was driven by our differing perspectives, and I fought to convince Aaron how right I was.

Pride told me that I deserved more than fearing for my life or my future and that I was worthy of more. That line of thinking sowed *another* seed of dissatisfaction. I was disgusted at what our lives had become, unable to see how God was moving in us at all.

❀   ❀   ❀

Within a few hours of our leaving the gas station, someone from our church contacted us, shared how they heard of our need from the organization, and offered us a place to live. When we were without the power to do anything for ourselves, God came through and revealed Himself to us. In light of His goodness and provision, I was humbled and relieved. I thought about my harsh words to Aaron, feeling embarrassed for my lack of faith and lack of self-control. Yet in my pride, I chose not to apologize, pretending as if it had never happened at all.

Being homeless for a few worrisome hours was difficult for me to experience, but there was another aspect of marriage that was persistently challenging. Aaron and I were still having issues in the bedroom, residually affecting our whole lives. Since sex had been such an enormous struggle for us, small nuisances seemingly amplified. We often caught ourselves squabbling over the slightest disagreement.

The more we neglected sexual intimacy, the worse our attitudes grew toward each other. It was as if we were building walls in our hearts, keeping each other at a distance, rather than building a bridge between us. With each impenetrable wall we built, knowing each other in an intimate way became a more impossible challenge. After a few arguments erupted and were drawn out over several days, it dawned on me that our relationship seemed the most vulnerable when we went long periods without engaging in romance. However, even when I knew the root cause of our problems, I struggled to snap out of my poor attitude and redirect my energy and efforts toward building intimacy. Pride was the culprit, often elongating the fights we had. We were in a tug-of-war with our hearts, both of us clenching the rope tightly, motivated by self-preservation. During those times, we did not interact like a loving couple concerned about each other's welfare. Our love felt imprisoned by a conviction to withhold affection for ransom. I wanted to win, I wanted to be right, I wanted validation. *I, I, I!*

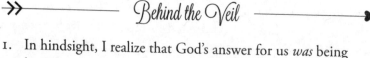

Behind the Veil

1. In hindsight, I realize that God's answer for us *was* being homeless, using our situation to prune us of pride. God

wanted us to rely on Him and not our flesh; to trust in His timing. That is a lesson we continue to encounter to this day. Do you struggle with pride? In what ways do you believe God has revealed a heart of pride in you? How has God used the circumstances you and your husband have faced to remove that pride from the two of you?

2. A lack of intimacy contributes to erosion in any marriage, and the disconnection gives room for nasty attitudes to arise. In what ways does a lack of intimacy affect your attitude and ultimately your marriage?

3. I never thought I struggled with pride. But once I became a wife, the validation I needed from my husband increased and intensified. I needed to know that my husband knew how I felt *at all times*, and I wanted him to affirm *me*. When he failed to meet my expectations, I withheld my love and affection intentionally and pridefully, until he satisfied my need for affirmation. How do you seek validation from your husband? What consequences are there if he doesn't meet your expectations? Why is it dangerous to rely fully on receiving validation from your husband, even more than from God?

4. Aaron and I were on a wild ride together with God. Some days were really fun and full of laughter as we explored Florida, while other days had us shaken up as trials thrashed about like a hurricane. Balancing my emotions and attitudes became a challenge. Do you find it difficult to accept that you and your husband can simultaneously experience good times and difficult ones? If so, why? And how do expectations play a role in your responses to different circumstances?

CHAPTER 16

Escape Artists

Aaron and I had been married a year and a half when some friends invited us to join them in Canada to help start a nonprofit organization. After much prayer and deliberation, we decided to accept their offer and move from Florida. Although we felt God guiding us to partner with our friends there, we were also good at escaping present pains. The trouble we experienced sexually was wreaking havoc on other aspects of our relationship: No matter how good things might have been, that one aspect seemed to overshadow all the good.

Instead of hyperfocusing on our intimacy issue, however, I found many other things to complain about, projecting my frustration onto smaller issues like work, volunteering, finances, or friendships. Once again I clung to the idea that if Aaron and I had a fresh start in a new place, maybe—just maybe—things would change for the better. Even if things didn't, the excitement of moving and experiencing something new would numb the pain just enough to carry me through the drought.

Aaron and I traveled an insane number of miles in that early part of our marriage. We were mission-minded and mobile, ready for any adventure God had for us, eager to remain in a constant state of distraction and stimulation. Driving north to Canada was one of my favorite road trips with Aaron. On our way up the East Coast we stopped in Washington, DC; we drove through New York City traffic; and we saw friends in Virginia, Connecticut, and upstate New York. We covered many miles of asphalt before arriving at the border. Our destination was Thousand Islands, a beautiful area north of Syracuse and south of Ottawa.

As we crossed a major bridge into Canada, I was astonished to see the marvelous view. A portion of a large river ran beneath us, winding around countless small islands. Some of the islands were covered with trees; others had houses built right on the shoreline. The river was just a part of the water system running through the Thousand Islands, and the place we were headed sat on the banks of one of the many channels.

Our directions led us off a main road and onto a dirt path. Tall Canadian trees lined the mile-long driveway. As the trees began to thin out, we finally spotted the house. We had seen a few pictures of it, but it was even better than we'd imagined. Our friends owned the property and let us stay in the guesthouse that sat adjacent to the main home. We lugged our belongings upstairs into a spacious loft with an exhilarating view of the water directly in front of where the bed sat.

While I stood at the window and gazed at the sparkling river, Aaron dropped some luggage next to the bed and walked over to me. He put his arms around me as we stared out the window.

I thanked God for leading us there and prayed that this would be the change we needed to inspire a better sex life. Prior to this move we hadn't lived in a place of our own, except for the few months we'd spent in Washington State and then the semi-private tent we'd occupied in Africa; so for almost two years we had lived with families and friends. This guesthouse was just as good as having our own apartment, and it didn't take long for Aaron and me to feel settled in.

I felt energized to collaborate with our friends, as well as to experience the world around us. We kayaked, fished, chopped wood, and visited local churches. Amid the adventures, I was eager to help our friends see their vision become a reality. For two months, Aaron and I spent hours working alongside this couple, giving me ample time to get to know them better.

❀   ❀   ❀

One day my friend and I found ourselves in a deep conversation regarding marriage. For some reason, I was able to be vulnerable and felt comfortable enough to share with her the struggle Aaron and I faced with sex. This was the first time I truly opened up and unveiled myself to another since becoming a wife.

She gave me a few things to consider. Some things I had heard before, such as setting the mood, but then she asked me if I had an intimate relationship with God. No one had ever asked me that before. I'd never even felt a reason to *ask myself* that question. Of course I felt like I was close to God: I prayed and read the Bible just about every day . . . *but was it intimate?* I would like to think it was, despite blaming Him for not making my marriage fulfilling. But was I being truthful?

I spent a few days pondering her question. I had always associated the word *intimacy* with *sex*, so I needed to fully comprehend intimacy's meaning before I could evaluate my relationship with God. I went online to the Merriam-Webster dictionary site and typed in *intimacy*. It read: "(1) the state of being intimate: familiarity; (2) something of a personal or private nature."[4] Then I typed in *intimate,* and it stated: "belonging to or characterizing one's deepest nature" and "marked by a warm friendship developing through long association."[5]

I stared at the screen and wondered, *Am I intimate with God?* Deep down I knew the answer: definitely not like I could be, like I should be. I had things that I prayed about from time to time and I felt comfortable praying out loud, whether by myself or with others. I worshiped God and sang to Him often. I was familiar with God's Word and I served Him faithfully. But something was missing. For the most part I had locked up my experiences and emotions in the recesses of my heart. I rarely, if ever, willingly gave God the access into my heart that intimacy requires.

Why? I was scared of what He would see. I was scared to face those things myself, and I was scared of having to let go and resolve them. Fear kept my relationship with God just barely below the surface. I realized that I had put up a wall in my heart to protect myself from getting hurt. My parents' divorce had left me with emotional wounds, and I was afraid of being hurt like that in any future relationship. My defense mechanism was so deeply ingrained that it had become an automatic response to any potential conflict or threat.

For the first time, I was confronted with the truth that I kept all of my relationships at a distance, including my relationship with Aaron, and more important, my relationship with God. I had experienced moments when I had allowed those barriers to come down a bit, but I never understood why or how it happened.

As I struggled with this new realization, another thought challenged me: *If a woman cannot experience intimacy with God, how much more will she struggle to experience intimacy with her husband?*

This was a powerful correlation between the two most important relationships in my life. With this new comprehension of the word *intimacy*, and the suggestion of a correlation between my relationship with God and my husband, I had some searching to do. It was uncomfortable knowing that I needed to be more intimate with God, but I also had a strong desire to be at that personal place with Him. I dedicated more time to reading Scriptures, and I began to pray more intently, talking to God more honestly and openly about things I was dealing with.

Since God is all knowing, it seemed silly to share with Him my worries or cares, but I did it, pursuing a deeper connection with my heavenly Father. I wanted to make myself known to Him, holding nothing back. As I committed to a more intimate relationship with God, I hoped my intimacy with my husband would naturally increase.

❋　❋　❋

Aaron and I did experience more intimacy. We shared the warmth of friendship, and we got to know each other on a deeper level. Our conversations became a little more open and we let ourselves laugh more, even during hardships. When we were intimate sexually, we found ways to make our time together pleasurable, and we learned how to communicate our way through it.

Although talking about sex with others had always been difficult for me, talking about it with my husband was even tougher. Yet I was slowly learning that being respectful of each other's sexual boundaries, opinions, and preferences provided us the freedom to explore and communicate during sex. As we pursued intimacy, we found a glimmer of hope for our marriage. It felt good to connect with my husband over the very issue that was suffocating the life out of us—to break down the barrier of fear that I had lived behind for so long.

While I was not able to overcome fear completely, I could handle it enough to navigate and address important issues with God and my husband. By doing so, I realized it was not embarrassing to let them know me, nor was I judged for the opinions or emotions I had tied to these issues. With each courageous step I took to communicate—to unveil—I learned more about myself and the fears that held me back from experiencing true intimacy. For example, as I shared with God how I was feeling about sex, I sensed Him telling me that I needed to let go of my expectations so that I didn't feel pressured to perform, which had left me feeling severely burdened. The fear of not doing the right thing or not being sexy enough had haunted me and ultimately made me uninterested in putting myself under such high stress.

I didn't really know how to strip my mind of those expectations—I had never even acknowledged them before—but I tried to rely less on what I thought our experiences together *should* be like and to joyfully embrace whatever unfolded each night. Judging by the look of ecstasy on Aaron's face once I'd adopted that attitude, he was surprised that I was able to keep smiling though we were not yet experiencing full intercourse. I no longer let disappointment steal those intimate moments from us as I had grown used to doing, I didn't say anything negative, and I didn't cry about it. I let the night progress with whatever we could do and let that be enough. Aaron seemed much more satisfied, thanking me more than once for a fun time together.

When I stopped comparing my marriage to the expectations I held, it suddenly became okay that we were struggling in this area. Every night was not perfect, but I was practicing this new approach, believing God would help me transform my expectations of sex and intimacy. I still encountered pain during sex, so we became intentional about pleasing each other in other ways. With a fresh breath of air sustaining me, we slowly moved forward.

⊛   ⊛   ⊛

Our time in Canada did not last as long as we thought it would. The paperwork to get the new nonprofit off the ground would take a minimum of nine months to process. In the meantime, our savings account had been depleted, and Aaron's deferred school loans were about to be reinstated. If we were to stay in Canada, our only option would be to rely fully on our friends' income. Aaron and I took everything into account, submitted it before the Lord, and asked Him to lead us.

Near the end of October, I told Aaron that I felt the Lord urging us to go back home. I told him that I had a different feeling from what I'd encountered on the way to Latin America the year before. This prompting was not just about my desire to see my family; rather, it came with much more peace. When I expressed my thoughts on God leading us to Southern California, Aaron responded by saying he had the exact same notion. As we prayed earnestly about the decision, we both felt God definitely directing us toward home.

We'd covered more than five thousand miles across North America in our small car, and now we loaded it up before adding a few more. Although it was bittersweet leaving such a phenomenal place and a potential ministry with our friends, the peace we had about going home was undeniable. Now all we had to figure out was *why* was God moving us home?

On the long trek west, Aaron and I talked about all the benefits of living in our hometown again, narrowing it to a few specific goals we felt God asking of us: to spend quality time with family and to achieve financial freedom. We talked about the importance of being debt-free and brainstormed ways we could pay off Aaron's school loan as soon as we possibly could. Aaron mentioned his ability to do side work as a photographer for a former employer, and I scrolled through my contacts to see how many babysitting jobs I could land. I knew our plans could change once we got home, but we grew excited talking about our talents and how we could use them to get ahead.

As Aaron drove, I stared out the window in deep thought. This move was different for me than the others had been. The earlier decisions I'd helped make to relocate always came with a longing to keep our relationship alive, despite the fizzle evident in the romance department. I never talked to Aaron about any underlying motive, but together we chased after incredible opportunities to experience more, thus avoiding ever really feeling anything was lacking in our relationship. I don't know about Aaron, but many of my choices to keep moving were heavily influenced by the belief that a new place would help heal us, or keep us so distracted we would stay together.

With this move home, I gained confidence in the bedroom because I had discovered the difference between intimacy and sex, and I was learning how to communicate to my husband about both. I was more content than I had ever been in our marriage. Going home would not mean trying to escape to an exciting new place to revitalize us. On the contrary, we were intentional about acknowledging that this move was going to be hard work.

As these thoughts came flooding in, God spoke softly to me—I knew it was Him because I had never thought about my marriage this way. He showed me how my husband and I had a tendency to escape our pain through the next big adventure. It wasn't wrong for us to look forward to the future or to base our decisions on multiple factors, but God wanted me to see a greater message. It was imperative that we faced our struggles with faithfulness and were aware of how those struggles dictated what we did. More than working hard to achieve financial freedom, I hoped this move meant God would also use this opportunity to help me face our marital struggles and heal us. I didn't know what that would look like, but I wanted it! I longed to have a healthy marriage in which we would bless each other and honor God.

Behind the Veil

1. My passion to serve God outweighed my desire to escape my marital problems, but at the core of my heart, both influenced and helped me justify the decisions I made with my husband. As tempting as it may be to chase after adventure for the mere experience, when we use those opportunities as a means of distraction, our spirit suffers. No matter how extraordinary the opportunity, dissatisfaction creeps in and causes contention. Running away or escaping pain is damaging as those wounds become infected and thus turn into an even greater problem later. Is there any issue that you have avoided or tried to escape? If so, what is it? Why do you believe running away is the best choice?

2. Learning the difference between intimacy and sex was vital to my perspective on marriage. I was convinced intimacy

revolved around sex. But I discovered intimacy and sex weren't the same thing. Knowing I could be deeply intimate with *God* was difficult for me to grasp as I was raised believing I knew God well, and applying such wisdom would take years for me to fully comprehend. Have you struggled to rightly define intimacy and sex? How does knowing the two are different ways to connect in marriage change your outlook on your relationship with your husband? Would you describe your relationship with God as intimate?

3. I found it challenging to talk to my husband about sex, especially *during* sex. Yet we were reaching a comfortable place in our relationship, and becoming aware of each other's likes and dislikes was significant to how we fulfilled each of our needs. Do you feel comfortable talking to your husband about sex? Why or why not?

4. Acknowledging that my parents' divorce affected me even into adulthood was a breakthrough. My heart broke when I realized I had kept my relationships at a distance, and I wanted to let down that barrier. Have you been keeping God or your husband at a distance? What are some reasons you might be doing this?

CHAPTER 17
Dark Days

I was hopeful that when we moved home, Aaron and I would be able to work everything out. I would grow as a Christ-follower and as a wife. I would never again fall into despair or depression. Finally everything would click for me, healing would come swiftly, and the revelations I received from God on that long drive to California would change my *entire* life.

But as I am human and weak in spirit, that was not the case. As I yearned to gain deeper intimacy with God and with my husband, the enemy was quick to retaliate against me and any progress I made. The more I showed zeal for God and attempted to draw close to Him, the more resistance I met through an onslaught of temptation, sin, frustration, and darkness. And once again when discontentment knocked at my heart's door, instead of remembering how much closer Aaron and I had grown and how much God had worked in my life, I chose to give in to irritation and dissatisfaction.

We had been in our hometown four months. Since part of our goal was to pay off our debt and get a stronger financial standing, we opted to live with my mom and stepdad. I quickly found a job as a preschool teacher's assistant, but it took Aaron six weeks to land a secure job. Once we were both working steadily, we put aside 10 percent for God, paid low rent, budgeted a small amount for food and gas, then spent the remaining money to pay off Aaron's school loans. Our "plan" was in full effect.

Being surrounded by familiarity was comforting and discouraging at the same time. The friends we thought we'd reconnect with seemed uninterested and disconnected, and we didn't have a church to attend. Gaining our bearings financially, socially, and intimately was going to take much more work than I was prepared for. Without a solid support system to encourage us to fight for our goals and to keep us accountable and spiritually strong, I felt cracks begin to break up our foundation.

I thought that returning to school—which would fulfill my parents' dream for my future—would help strengthen my resolve. But the truth was that I was running again, longing to escape.

Weariness settled in my heart, stealing my joy. I had not yet received the healing to enjoy intercourse. I had been holding on for six months since the revelation I encountered in Canada. Despite my efforts to remain faithful, intense anger burned inside me. And the relationship with God that had been so sweet turned bitter yet again. I felt like I was on a seesaw of emotions—I trusted God and knew He would work everything out for our good, and then I deeply distrusted Him and grew distant. But this time I seemed to fall harder than I ever had. I blatantly ignored God and refused to attend church. I created any excuse not to make it to a Sunday morning service.

I also became acutely aware that Aaron had stopped pursuing me romantically; I knew it wasn't simply because we were living with my mom and stepdad. I knew it was because I had again become reluctant to have sex. And when he stopped pursuing me, my heart turned cold—although I was also relieved that we didn't have to *try* as often. In an effort to escape reality, ditch spending time with my husband, and avoid attending church on Sundays, I dove into my responsibilities as a student. I figured my school projects and homework assignments would give me the reasonable excuses I thought I needed.

For the first time, I wasn't actively participating in church. I felt the effects of it immediately, such as allowing my flesh to give in to temptation and giving my attitude free rein, but I was too proud to submit to God. What made me feel worse was that although I knew Aaron had to be upset about our marriage, he never turned his back on God. He may have compromised Sunday mornings for a while, but he often went to a service for young adults during the week. He attended while I was in class or doing homework. Knowing that my husband was still passionate about God stirred my anger all the more. I wondered, *How can he honor God when God is withholding His power to heal us, His children?* I was also jealous that Aaron could genuinely experience intimacy with God, knowing full well I was missing out.

⊛　⊛　⊛

During the months that followed, Aaron and I engaged in sexual intimacy only a few times. We would "try" to have sex, but nothing ever came of it. Sometimes a whole month or two would pass without us being physically affectionate at all. We didn't intentionally deny each other, we just did not feel close anymore. We had become merely roommates. Our friendship was even beginning to deteriorate, and I didn't know how to stop it from waning.

One day Aaron invited me to go with him to check out the married couples' community at church. He had mentioned it a few times before, but I always declined. Knowing we could not continue as we were, and desiring restoration, I finally said yes. We walked in, hoping to slip into the crowd without anyone noticing. Being invisible was next to impossible as the room was filled to capacity and the majority of the couples were much older than we were. As we stood there, I was overcome with apprehension. We glanced around the room and then I motioned to him to turn around, with every intention of walking out.

Just then a heavy hand landed on my shoulder as I heard a man's voice joyfully welcoming us and asking if we were new. We said yes and the man, Tom, did not hesitate to make room for us at his table with his wife and a few other couples. I was embarrassed to watch people scoot over for us, especially with the service about to begin. That night was socially awkward for me. I had no idea what these other marriages were enduring, but from my perspective, they seemed perfect. *I* wanted perfect. Inside I was crying out for everyone to see that we needed help, but I sat quietly, afraid to utter a single word.

Surprisingly, Aaron and I left that night feeling a sense of connection restored. We talked about our experience and how it felt good to be in the presence of other married couples. We went back the next week and the week after that. Each Wednesday night we drove to the church my husband had been attending solo. I found it refreshing to be surrounded by couples who shared honestly and openly about their marriages and what God was teaching them.

Although attending that group was a bright spot in our week, my husband and I fought constantly, especially every Wednesday night right before we headed to church. It seemed as though any time we submitted to God and allowed Him to guide us, both our flesh and the enemy of our souls attacked as forcibly as they could. Our romance was a tragedy, our marriage was suffering, and I felt trapped. It seemed as though I couldn't even make it a week. After every Wednesday night marriage meeting, I'd feel hope and would determine to press on in my fight for my marriage. But by Thursday, I'd be consumed with frustration and hopelessness.

I ate comfort food to help alleviate the pain, but it merely resulted in thirty extra pounds to carry around, continuing the vicious cycle of my battle with depression. I dyed my hair close to black, even though I grew up blonde. The awkwardness of my outward unattractiveness was a reflection of what I was internalizing.

I never would have imagined that my marriage would reach such a dispiriting condition. Our struggles definitely were not part of my plan. Even though I knew the only way to break free from my misery was to seek God and surrender myself to Him, for some reason I just couldn't. I resisted out of resentment, justifying my feelings. I was raised knowing God, I abstained from sex, my husband also kept himself pure, we dated with boundaries for the most part, we submitted our relationship to God, we got married, and we dove into serving as a team to further the Kingdom—we "did all the right things." And God failed to reward us. It just wasn't fair. My mind was stuck on performance, believing that striving for perfection guaranteed blessing.

I wondered over and over, *Why would the God we so fervently follow keep our marriage from being fulfilled?* I was blinded by hurt and could not comprehend why God would not just provide us with some sort of miracle. Yet instead of asking God for that kind of help, I gave up. Night after night Aaron would pray for us before we went to bed. Sometimes he would ask me to pray, but I usually declined. Acknowledging God made me sad, and talking to Him through prayer was overwhelming. The little girl who knew God and spent her life following Him, the one wanting to believe wholeheartedly in His mighty plan, had become a stranger to me. I didn't know who I was anymore.

Behind the Veil

1. Looking back, I am in awe at the way God orchestrates things so perfectly. God pursued my husband and me amid our pain and anger. He put the call in our hearts to attend the marriage group that first Wednesday night. To say that I was terrified of stepping one foot in that church is an understatement. What I discovered once there surprised me. The couples we met inspired us to have a better marriage and to seek consistently after God. They even encouraged us to sit with them on Sunday mornings at church. We decided to make more of an effort to go as often as we could, and our new friends held us accountable in our attendance.

Are there situations, such as attending church or marriage counseling, that you have avoided because of anger or fear? If so, did you end up going? What was your motivation? Was there a positive outcome you are thankful for?

2. In my depression, my outward appearance became an expression of my inner strife. I did not look like myself anymore. I was spiraling out of control, eating to numb my emotional pain, feeling unattractive and unhealthy, fueling a desire to eat more, resulting in gaining more. I was searching for happiness instead of God, but my way of doing so only provided brief and fleeting moments of joy. What do you do when you're searching for happiness? Do you binge on food, alcohol, shopping, or something else? When you do this your way instead of seeking true joy in God, how does that affect your intimate relationship with God? With your husband?

3. I questioned God many times about the suffering I experienced in my marriage, failing to stop and listen to Him or search His Word for truth. It was a stretch for me even to contemplate the idea that God could be more concerned with my character than my comfort. What circumstances have led you to question God? Did you try to understand His perspective?

CHAPTER 18

The Blame Game

❧

A sweet-and-savory aroma had warmly invited us into our friend's quaint little home. My husband joined the men outside around the barbecue, while I sat with the women around the kitchen island. Our ages and life stages varied, but we were friends, brought together because of our faith and our wife-hood. Beautiful voices chirped back and forth in conversation, sharing stories from earlier that day. With the natural progression of any group of women, we continued to talk as one tangent led to another, covering a wide array of topics including home decor and essentials. The other wives happily boasted about the best quality kitchen rugs, the perfect measuring cups, and the pros and cons of different coffeemakers. Unbeknownst to them, their innocent chatter began to make me feel insecure and inadequate. My eyes drifted away from the women, only to be overcome with grief after seeing all kinds of fun appliances and cookware overflowing from the countertops. It wasn't their fault; my emotions had been build-ing for some time. I let my mind fester with negative thoughts, spoiling my evening.

All I could think about was the fact that I didn't have any of the things they discussed. I couldn't contribute to the conversation without having those household necessities, so I kept to myself.

I kept the burden of inadequacy and discontentment tucked away, knowing eventually it would seep out in my responses toward my husband. For some reason, I was okay with that, as if he were the only one to blame.

We had eagerly pursued a mission to be debt-free—a plan we'd agreed on together but that at times left us divided. In an effort to put as much money as possible toward our debt, we decided to extend our stay with my mom and stepdad. Although our housing situation was comfortable, I was filled to the brim with discontentment. I wanted my *own* place with my *own* things to fill it with. I didn't care that we were aggressively chipping away at our debt. I knew we were diligently being good stewards with our finances, but still I could only dwell on all the different items that money could have been used for, which I was convinced would heal my heart, relieve my anxiety, and provide a place where I could prove myself as a wife, whether hosting friends or serving my husband. If we lived on our own, I made myself believe, then our struggle with sex would clear up and we wouldn't fight as much. Life would be perfect.

Over the course of almost two years in California, our problems mounted. I put the weight of frustration from the challenges we faced sexually, financially, and spiritually into a funnel, reasoning with my husband that the only way to fix our issues was to have our own home. My husband, a logical man, tried to explain to me the impact of the recession, the consequences of debt, and the implications of how much it would actually take to invest in our own home. As he reminded me of our plan, he also told me he wasn't against the idea completely; he just wanted us to wait until we were debt-free and had saved some money. To me, however, it only felt like he was pushing back. So I pushed harder.

It's your fault we are even in this mess.
The debt isn't mine, it's all yours. They're your school loans.
What you spend on your debt, I should get to spend on what
*   I want.*

I really wish you didn't bring this debt into our marriage.
It's your debt, your problem.

The rude and disrespectful thoughts turned to snide comments, all resting on my husband's shoulders. In every argument, I used whichever one would be the most provoking to get my point across. We had already endured so much torture in the intimacy department, and we'd faced many trials overseas. We had followed God as He directed our moves around North America, and we'd dealt with character challenges that seemed to rise up daily. Now it felt as if our money was being confiscated too.

The more I blamed my husband or God, the more justified I felt, trying to convince myself I was still "good." I refused to take responsibility for anything that happened, which only fed my pride and hardened my heart. This lethal combination of negative emotion and retreat from my husband led to more sin, more hurt, and more marital erosion. I realize now that I may never have recognized my deep-seated sin if I had not said yes to becoming a wife. In the middle of blaming my husband, or during a fight or a situation I was unhappy about, my husband would point out one of the deadliest sins I harbored, revealed as it erupted through my responses: manipulation.

❀   ❀   ❀

One day, feeling particularly emotional, I walked out on Aaron, marched into our bedroom, and slammed the door. I knew that action would physically separate us and emotionally sever us. My husband had made it clear to me early in our relationship that he did not like me turning my back on him in a conversation, so I intentionally slammed it. I wanted him to know how angry I was and how sorry he should be for making me feel that way.

He pushed the door back open and stared angrily at me. After a few seconds of staring each other down, he spoke firmly. "Why did you shut the door?"

I wanted to ignore him. I wanted to run again and slam another door to separate us—but this time not out of anger or frustration, but because embarrassment overwhelmed me.

"Why did you shut the door?" Aaron repeated.

"Because I'm mad! You frustrate me and I can't take it anymore." I tried to be just as firm, but I knew what I had done was wrong.

"I know you know how much it hurts me when you walk away like that, and slamming the door on top of that is like spitting in my face. You chose to do something that you *knew* would hurt me. And you did it to try to manipulate the situation."

Hating that he called my sin by name, I shot back, "It is not manipulation! I was just frustrated, and I need a break from the crazy."

"It *is* manipulation when you do something you know will hurt me," Aaron said. "You want me to feel like you are feeling." Tears filled his eyes. "You blame me for everything! You want me to apologize regardless of who is at fault, you refuse to acknowledge that you do anything wrong, and you do things to hurt me and justify it as though you need to teach me a lesson. What you are doing is unacceptable."

As my husband clearly communicated how he felt, I began to understand that my manipulation was more than precise words said with impeccable timing. It was laced through my body language, which spoke volumes. I had convinced myself I wasn't manipulating him, but rather was justified in my actions. The truth was that I wanted to control my husband, to get him to do something I wanted him to do or to make him hurt like I hurt.

Turning away from Aaron was a tactic I used to let him know how serious I was. I knew he found this act intolerable, but that never stopped me. In fact I kept that knowledge in my back pocket just in case we ever fought and I needed an extra round of ammunition to fire back. Too many times I turned my back on him in anger, ignored his texts, left his calls unanswered, hung up on him, slammed the door, and walked away. I did these things intentionally. In the heat of our arguments, I wanted the quarrel and the pain to stop, but I didn't want to surrender. I didn't think I needed to be part of the solution, because from my point of view, I wasn't part of the problem.

I knew the deep wounds I could inflict on my husband by my actions of turning from him. And yet despite that knowledge, I deliberately decided to do it anyway. Deciding not to care was a dangerous place to be. Instead of describing to him how I felt and talking my way through marital issues, I chose to communicate with him in a way that was destructive.

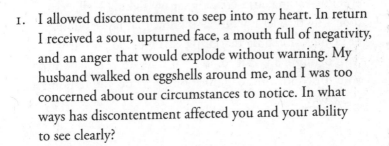

Behind the Veil

1. I allowed discontentment to seep into my heart. In return I received a sour, upturned face, a mouth full of negativity, and an anger that would explode without warning. My husband walked on eggshells around me, and I was too concerned about our circumstances to notice. In what ways has discontentment affected you and your ability to see clearly?

2. Certain triggers fed my growing discontentment, including seeing happy couples, decorated homes, and successful people sharing epic stories. In the presence of such beautiful things, all I could see was my lack. What are some things that trigger discontentment for you? Why do you think it is important to be aware of these triggers?

3. Whenever I felt unsatisfied, I blamed my husband. It didn't take long for anything and everything to be his fault. Just as Adam blamed Eve in the Garden and then Eve blamed the serpent, I pointed my finger and blamed my husband. To be honest, I shamefully admit I still tend to do this in

my weakness. I am learning how to be humble and take
responsibility, but I struggle with emotional resistance
because deep down I don't want any failures or problems
to be my fault. In what situations have you blamed your
husband for something that was either partly or all because
of you? What are some words that describe why you blamed
your husband instead of assuming responsibility?

4. I used to think manipulation was a way people twisted their
words to justify their perspective. I thought it was a strategy
reserved for malicious people, never giving any thought
to the idea that I was someone who did this. However,
when I became a wife I realized I used manipulation often.
Manipulation can be exercised through words, but it also
happens through body language. Eye-rolling, condescending
eyebrow-raising, arm-crossing, heavy sighing—all were
tools I used to let my husband know that he was doing
or saying something that displeased me. Do you struggle
with manipulation? If so, in what ways do you respond to
your husband with manipulation? Why do you respond in
those ways?

CHAPTER 19
Fantasyland

During this dark period, Aaron and I fell into a habit of watching TV and movies. Diving into a fantasy world seemed to briefly relieve the burden destroying us. Although we sat next to each other, we were worlds apart. The thought of divorce, which I was so adamantly against, was contaminating our love. At one point I told Aaron I felt guilty that he was not being fulfilled sexually and I wouldn't be upset if he wanted out. I even begged him to divorce me, encouraging him to find a satisfying life elsewhere. His initial response was an absolute no, but he did share with me later that he was threatened with the thought of divorce as well. As much as I may have contemplated divorce, my soul was convicted not to go that route. We did love each other, but hanging on to threads of memories of the good times was barely enough to keep our hearts knit together.

Our three-year anniversary was supposed to be celebratory. I assumed most couples would plan an adventurous getaway, a romantic dinner, or some other exciting date to commemorate three years of joy together, yet our anniversary was a disturbing reminder of how long we had continued without sex. Our struggle was not something we could laugh at, hoping it would work itself out soon. How could we possibly celebrate, when mourning seemed more appropriate?

I grieved the death of my marriage as if it were already gone. The lens I viewed my world through was tinted and cloudy, keeping me from seeing or thinking clearly. My thoughts began to disturb me: scenarios of my husband tragically dying, giving me the option to meet someone new. I never wished such severe things to really happen, but I was often tempted to escape into a fantasy world to avoid what I was dealing with in reality.

⊛　⊛　⊛

I enjoyed fantasyland. I seemed to get carried away in another realm that satisfied my desires better than the truth of what I was facing. During that time I picked up the book *Twilight*. Within a few weeks I was spending any free time I had reading the series. I dove into the odd relationship between Edward and Bella, eager to see how life turned out for them. Aside from my responsibilities and my reading, I checked out. I did not mind hiding myself within the pages of the Twilight books; in fact I became obsessed with them. I joined in the conversations at work regarding anything Twilight, and I followed any trending topics related to the saga, including movie productions and any news of the actors and actresses who played in them. The books, the characters, and even the movie stars playing out the drama became my idols.

I found temporary diversion from emotional pain the more I believed in Twilight. I became fixated on the twisted love between the characters, and I became infatuated with the idea of Edward. Although I knew he was a fictional character, Edward somehow became my idol. I wanted to know him, I wanted to experience the love he had for Bella; meanwhile my husband sat right next to me as I turned each page. My perspective became skewed; my expectations for my husband rose higher, and when I stepped out of the false reality of Twilight, my marital issues amplified.

As I happily fell victim to this Twilight phenomenon, my

marriage was on the verge of collapse. Our emotions were bursting at the seams, and sadness turned into hopelessness, which turned into bitterness. I doubled down on avoiding God because I felt He had abandoned me. I was trusting Him to reconcile Aaron and me on my timeline, and it wasn't happening.

I did not see it right away, but there came a point when I realized my obsession with Twilight had become a sin. Idolizing the strange love story of Edward and Bella made my unhappiness and discontentment grow without restraint. I unleashed these negative emotions on my husband on a whim or I intentionally avoided him. I even compared our love to fiction. It didn't matter that Edward and Bella were *make believe*; Aaron was supposed to love me like Edward loved Bella. *I* was supposed to have that love story.

One day while chatting with a coworker about Twilight, feeding my craving for more, it dawned on me that I was not the saga's only victim. This young girl was wrapped up in the series, and I sensed she too was using it to escape the pain of her reality. I saw a reflection of myself in her. I blinked a few times and suddenly snapped out of my trance. Not only was I damaging my life by dwelling deep in the pages of these books, but I was contributing to other people's obsessions by feeding the conversation. I needed to pull in the reins on my infatuations, my expectations, and my fear of facing problems in my marriage, but I didn't know how.

My depression had been leading me to make decisions that fed my insecurity. Something had to give, so I stopped feeding my fantasies and attempted to focus on reality. It was a daily battle. When the conversations ran in circles around Bella and Edward, I had to keep my mouth shut or excuse myself. I talked myself out of caring about the movies or the actors in the series, replacing those thoughts with reminders that my husband is a good man and revisiting the reasons we fell in love. Doing this was not easy, but the more I redirected my attention from my fantasy world to Aaron, the easier it became the next time I was tempted.

❀ ❀ ❀

Coming to terms with the truth that I needed to put effort into being a good wife, an honorable wife, was painful. I despised seeing parts of myself that were not perfect—the sin-tainted actions that led me down a path of brokenness.

Although my flesh had been aggressively fighting with God and my husband for more than a year, gradually Aaron and I spent more time in church and made friends with other Christian couples. One husband and wife in particular, Chris and Joanne, made a huge impact on us. They led our marriage community group on Wednesday nights during the first few months we attended. Their funny banter back and forth revealed characteristics that Aaron and I found relatable and trustworthy. Some nights were harder to sit through than others, specifically when the topic highlighted sex. Couples would toss around jokes about the taboo church table talk to lighten the atmosphere, but for me it aroused uncomfortable feelings. While other couples laughed in agreement, Aaron and I just glanced at each other with tears in our eyes.

One Wednesday after service we pulled the leaders aside to share with them a little about our intimacy crisis. I suppose getting acquainted and committing to participate in this marriage community was a step toward bringing down those barriers in my heart, the ones built by fear and insecurity. Chris and Joanne were confounded by our story and invited us to their house later that week to talk more in depth about the issue.

I was nervous about approaching this couple, despite knowing their openness about sex. I wanted to back out several times, scared of how the conversation might go. No matter how many ways I thought about canceling, my husband's joy at the prospect of friendship and counseling was obvious as he shared his excitement with me. I didn't want to let him down again. Aaron and I desperately needed to find *some* kind of healing. I needed to find a solution to our problems before I lost my mind and our relationship.

We went to their house for dinner, anxious to get to the part where we would share the details of our whole story. This was one of our first experiences as a couple of being truly unveiled with others. Chris and Joanne listened intently. They did not hesitate to ask questions and even intentionally pry. Both of them took turns explaining things that might work to help our situation.

Instead of mentioning the things we had heard over and over from well-meaning people, Joanne talked about a friend who decided to switch all of her household products to organic in an effort to clear up some symptoms she was experiencing from polycystic ovary syndrome (PCOS). Within a short time her friend had ended up pregnant, something that was nearly impossible with her health condition.

Since I wasn't trying to get pregnant and I lacked the knowledge about the health benefits of using organic products, I disregarded the information.

I was sensitive that night, humiliated by how much personal information we had revealed. Yet for the first time, I had the opportunity to confront things we had never really addressed before, including things in our past.

Aaron and I had been honest about character flaws we saw in each other, gaining a better understanding of where we were and where we needed to be. I sat in Chris and Joanne's living room and wept. The reality that we were far from perfect and didn't have the perfect marriage was difficult for me to face. I cared too much about other people's perceptions of us, instead of being truthful with myself and working on things that needed major repair.

Chris and Joanne spent time praying over us, asking God to continue to speak to us, guide us, heal us, and bring us into a season of change. They blessed and affirmed us, specifically regarding our intimacy issues, and Joanne challenged me to invest in my marriage by gaining insight from others. Handing me my first marriage resource, *No More Headaches* by Dr. Juli Slattery, she encouraged me to read it, saying that it might radically alter the way I view sex. I left

Chris and Joanne's that night feeling invigorated, as though Aaron and I could actually be heading into a new season.

As we talked about the conversation we'd had with Chris and Joanne, I told Aaron that the way they looked at us as we shared our struggle with them touched my heart. Their glossy eyes were locked with ours, full of concern and love. I felt God looking through their eyes at us. It was reassuring to feel as though the God of the universe cared enough to sit with us in a living room and show us He cared for us, even when I had been so cold toward Him. Amid my stubborn and prideful tantrums, God reached out and loved me unconditionally. He was reminding me that He was aware of my burden and that He was a loving Father who desired for our marriage to be fulfilling.

This moment made my hard heart melt like ice cream on a warm summer day. I felt so terrible for neglecting God and being angry at Him. I even felt bad because, even in that heart-wrenching moment, parts of me still wrestled with pride. But I also encountered peace beyond understanding. I was able to look at my husband through the pain we had endured and love him still, to hang on and fight for what we had. That night we went to bed and prayed that the season of hardship we had endured and the depression I was suffering from was coming to an end.

$$\gg \text{——————} \quad \textit{Behind the Veil} \quad \text{——————} \rightarrow$$

1. Diving deep into the Twilight series and idolizing other love stories was harmful to my marriage. I experienced the pain of isolation as I emotionally severed myself from God and from my husband, feeding my flesh all the more. I became disgusted with myself, but I was afraid to face the reality of what my marriage had become and try to fix it. Have you ever tried to escape your marriage problems by seeking fulfillment in books, movies, or other types of fantasies? If

so, in what ways was your relationship with God or your husband affected?

2. I was fighting with God and with my husband daily. Yet even in my sin, God pursued me, putting people in my path who would reveal His great love for me! Are there ways God might be pursuing you, whether through a church invite or new friends? List all the ways God is showing you His great love. Does seeing that list soften your heart toward Him?

3. Unveiling myself before another couple caused me extreme anxiety. I didn't know if they would judge us, and I was terrified of people knowing that Aaron and I were not a happy couple. I only knew how to stuff my pain and hide from the world. Sitting in Chris and Joanne's house that evening changed everything, as my barriers gave way and parts of the real me trickled out. Relief filled my heart immediately. Have you resisted being transparent about the real you or the state of your marriage? If so, why? What thoughts go through your mind when you consider being real with others about your marital issues?

CHAPTER 20
Making Peace with My Past

<figure>ornamental flourish</figure>

Dusk was settling over the backyard. Aaron and I sat next to each other on a worn patio love seat. I was holding a glass of water in one hand and clasping Aaron's hand in the other. Laughter resonated as we broke the ice with the new family pastor and his wife, Bill and Michelle. We had invited ourselves over for dinner, hoping to build an authentic friendship with them. Knowing a little about their history, we also felt comfortable talking with them about our marriage, eager to see if they could assist us in growing as a husband and wife. Among the laughter and without going into great detail, I gathered up my courage and mentioned that we were struggling with intimacy and other marriage issues.

"How is your relationship with your dad?" Bill asked.

I was caught off guard by his question, uneasy about evaluating that specific relationship. In an instant, vulnerability brought a wave of emotion to the surface. Unveiling myself before others was not something I was exactly comfortable with, yet God kept giving me opportunities to do so. I knew this was one of those opportunities, so I took a deep breath and hesitantly shared about my childhood, the pain of my parents' divorce, and a pivotal moment from high school.

⊛   ⊛   ⊛

When I was very young, I had visitation with my dad every other weekend. It was never enough time. I was a daddy's girl without the consistency to really be a daddy's girl. I thought back to all the times I found myself jealous of family or friends who had special bonds with their dads. I yearned to have a stronger relationship with my dad. In fact, on visitation days I was so eager to see him, I sat in front of the window impatiently waiting for his car to pull in the drive. If he called to cancel, I composed myself long enough to act understanding on the phone, only to break down and cry when I hung up. I hated being from a divorced family, lacking the capacity to fully understand our family's new dynamic, which evolved and changed as I was growing up.

The summer before entering high school proved to be one of the most despairing periods of my life. I was left out of many details leading up to, and following through, what was happening between my mom and dad at the time, but I knew it revolved around a request for an increase in child support, and the court became involved. At one point my dad requested that my brother and I visit with him for a six-week stay during our summer break. All that resonated in my young, teenage heart was that I would be spending six weeks of my nine-week summer in a city I did not know well, away from all my friends. As much as I wanted to be close to my dad, thinking about how my summer would look seemed discouraging and really no fun. Halfway through that summer, my self-pity got the best of me. I missed my friends and all the comforts of life at my mom's house, and I protested.

In my disappointment and frustration over how I wanted to enjoy my summer, instead of talking through my feelings with my dad, I ran away from his house and called my mom to come get me and my twin brother, who had followed me for the sake of protection. While waiting for my mom, I saw my stepmother drive down the street searching for us. We hid so she wouldn't see us, but I could tell by her look that she was worried. My heart sank as I realized running away was not a good decision.

Feeling guilty, I called my stepmother to tell her where we were. She picked us up and drove us back to the house, where I continued to express my displeasure with the whole arrangement. It didn't take long for my mom to arrive at my dad's house. She explained that she was sorry, but I needed to stay with my dad because it was a court order. I wasn't happy and didn't know what I was going to do. Feeling forced to stay there did not feel good to me at all. I expressed my frustration through bouts of tears and talking to my brother about it when no one else was in the room. I became difficult and unwilling to "get with the program."

A few days later my dad came home from work and solemnly asked my brother and me to pack our bags. He didn't explain why we were leaving, only that we were going home.

The forty-minute drive back to my mom's house that night was full of sadness and uncertainty. I felt terrible for running away, ashamed of doing something outside my character. During the entire drive home, I wondered if I was the reason for the sudden change of plans. My insecurities flared up, feeding me all kinds of thoughts about how I was the source of the problem. My negative thoughts were only aggravated by how quiet everyone else was in the car.

Perhaps my dad didn't explain what was going on because he wasn't sure how to. Maybe he believed he was protecting us by not saying anything, or maybe he was dealing with his own insecurities as a parent and was challenged to process it all. The unfortunate thing is that by not saying what he was enduring, my immature imagination kicked into overdrive to fill in the gaps, leading me to conclude that *I* was a problem.

When we got to my mom's house, my dad took a moment to hug my brother and me. He told us, "I'm not sure when I will see you again, but I love you." I was relieved finally to be home, but my dad's words echoed in my heart as I tried to fall asleep that night. I wondered why he chose to say that to us, unable to fathom too much time passing until we saw each other again. I hoped the last few weeks were all a dream that I would wake up from soon.

My dad and I were standing on opposite sides of a chasm, unsure if our severed relationship would ever be mended. For almost two years I didn't hear from or see my dad. I often wondered during that time of absence about that summer and how things could have ended differently. I thought maybe my dad took us home that last night and stopped fighting to see us because he felt as if he needed to protect his new family from the chaos, and I believed I was getting in the way of that. To my teenage mind, it was difficult to see his love, pain, and insecurity. Instead I focused on my own. I fought feelings of abandonment, fear, and bitterness—all baggage that influenced who I was shaping up to be.

Despite the negativity that scarred my heart, I could not have been more excited to receive that first phone call from my dad after such a long time! Although I still felt angry and bitter toward him for choosing to avoid our relationship, the sense of relief that washed over me when I reconnected with him filled me with pure joy. We spent time catching each other up on what was going on in our lives, and we briefly talked about the two years of silence. Our first conversation barely covered any detail of the events that severed us, but I didn't push too hard with my questions because I was too excited to have my relationship with my dad back. I hoped to find out more as our relationship healed. I never found out why he called that day—and I didn't care. I was just glad to talk with him.

That call led to more calls and a more open relationship between us. Through our conversations, he made sure that I understood he wanted to make up for time lost—and I let him know I felt the same. While I knew that wasn't going to happen right away, I was thankful that God had brought us back together again. There were moments of awkwardness as we both offered and accepted apologies, but it was worth enduring the awkwardness, knowing we were both trying to mend the brokenness.

⊛ ⊛ ⊛

As I sat with Aaron, Bill, and Michelle, I revealed the impact my dad's action had on my life, even into adulthood. I dug deep into my heart and unearthed the bottled-up emotions I was still clinging to.

That night as I shared openly and honestly, I realized that much of my anger and bitterness stemmed from a lack of knowing my dad's perspective. All of a sudden it dawned on me that my dad was on a unique journey himself, and I had never considered his motives or how he truly felt about the challenges he faced. Up to this point, I expected my dad to be a perfect father, something no one can fulfill completely. By lowering my expectations of him and seeking to know him better, I hoped my relationship with him would improve.

"I haven't really thought about that summer until now," I told them. "I know it had a huge effect on me, but I'm not good at acknowledging why I feel certain things. Instead I just kept bottling up each emotion. No matter what happened during my childhood with my dad, I love him."

Bill encouraged me to confront those hurt feelings I had locked away. He said that if I could find healing and reconciliation with my dad, I might find it easier not to be so guarded with Aaron. He also explained how sometimes people can mold their perceptions of our heavenly Father based on our earthly fathers. I held on to this concept to evaluate how my relationships with God, my father, and my husband all impacted me.

Aaron and I were encouraged by the conversation that night. On our way home I could not stop thinking about my relationship with my dad.

Will things ever be complete between us? I wondered.

I knew I could be stubborn and prideful. If any length of

time went by without us communicating, I felt as though it was his responsibility to call me. Although I didn't know where that entitlement attitude came from, it definitely kept me from initiating in our relationship. The more time passed, the more bitter I became, justifying my withholding. I think a part of me also feared experiencing separation again, and I believed my dad should have acted swiftly to avoid such devastation. So when time lapsed and I didn't hear from him, I believed he just didn't care.

The same was true in my marriage, thinking that it was Aaron's responsibility to initiate intimacy with me, and until he did so, I'd hold back my affection. In fact, I realized that I also did this in my walk with God. I waited for Him to do what I wanted, standing at a distance and testing to see if there was any threat to my heart. I'd often run or withhold my attention and affection—my default defense mechanisms.

Why do I do this? Why do I convince myself that relationships will thrive without my participation? I started to ask myself over and over.

❀　❀　❀

Shortly after meeting with Bill and Michelle, I noticed it had been a few weeks since I had talked to my dad. I was confronted with a choice: to apply the relationship wisdom I had gained and call him, or ignore it and lean back on my old ways of waiting for him to initiate. In a moment of authentic repentance and in response to the Holy Spirit's conviction, I laid down my pride and called my dad. Evaluating the past and reflecting on my new revelations about my tendencies, I felt empowered to introduce the change I wanted to see in my relationship with him.

"Hello there, beautiful."

"Hi, Dad! How are you?"

"I'm doing great! I was just thinking about you."

A part of me struggled to receive that comment, as I thought, *If you were thinking about me, then why didn't you call?* But in an effort to change my perspective, I pushed aside my negativity and embraced what he said. As I did that and felt good knowing I was on his mind, I didn't know how to respond, I didn't know what all to share, or what would be interesting enough to keep him engaged in the conversation. In my awkwardness, I allowed a moment of silence.

Fortunately, my dad jumped in. "How is the photography business going? I heard you're going to Maui!"

"Yes, we're really excited to go, and I feel like it's going to be a good trip for Aaron and me. Thank you, by the way, for always sharing with people about our passion for photography. Without you we wouldn't be going on this trip!"

"You know I can't help it, Jen. You both are very talented."

"Thanks, Dad." Even though his compliments felt wonderful and I cherished them, I still felt another rush of awkward silence coming on.

"Hey, I need to get going, Dad. I was just calling to say hi."

"All right, darlin'. I love you. You're the best."

"Thanks, Dad. Love you too."

Although brief and slightly uncomfortable on my end, the conversation was a great one. That phone call made it easier to continue pursuing a better relationship with him, breaking the cycle of my stubbornness.

❀   ❀   ❀

I believe God used this situation to help heal my past. God brought to my attention again that for so long I'd bottled up my hurt feelings and let them rot on the shelves of my heart, and now it was time for me to remove some of the space-wasting clutter to make room for more joyful memories. Initiating in my relationship by simply making that call helped me see that my dad was human, just like me. He could sin, make mistakes, and let people down—all an inevitable by-product of living in a fallen world. I needed to accept this truth and stop allowing disappointment and fear to overcome me.

Slowly I was able to let go of the painful pieces of my parents' divorce, the resentment of not having a consistent and special "daddy's girl" bond with my dad, and the frustrations that built from a lack of understanding other people's perspectives. It is difficult to explain exactly how I did that, but it was as if my spirit opened my heart, grabbed those negative parts of my past, and handed them over to God. Then God took them from me, held my hands, and through His comfort healed me.

I also handed over my expectations of how I thought life should have turned out or how people should treat me, and I forgave my parents for their choices. I had to let go of the illusion of control I had clung to in a desperate attempt to protect myself, coming to terms with the reality that relationships will always involve risk. Yet in those precious and devastating moments of hardship, I knew that God's story of grace and redemption could prevail. I accepted the relationship I had with my dad, and I wanted that same fulfillment as a "daddy's girl" in my relationship with God. This process of handing God my past hurts, my expectations, and my fears did not occur in one single moment of prayer; rather it was a gradual change and continues to happen as I acknowledge those things I do not want taking up space in my heart.

The more I pondered the pastor's insight about how my relationship with my father could be affecting my marriage, the more I realized that remnants of other relationships will always find ways to creep into marriage, whether positive or negative. Now my responsibility was to evaluate my relationships and make sure I was doing my part to see them succeed, while also recognizing that I couldn't force anyone to meet my expectations. God was asking me to do my part, to love and forgive and apologize as needed, regardless of how others fulfill their part or even respond to me. God was teaching me how to be courageous, and in my obedience to Him, I began to experience extraordinary healing in those relationships. And it helped me see how I'd carried my wounds into my marriage and that they could wound Aaron as well.

>> ——————— *Behind the Veil* ———————➤

1. Throughout childhood and adolescence, many people and experiences influence and shape who we become as adults. Sometimes those events have major negative impacts on us that we are not even aware of! It is critical that we evaluate our hearts and confront issues from our past, which is the only way we'll reach true freedom and joy in marriage and other relationships. What was your childhood like? Are there any events that took place that may still affect you?

2. Being a "daddy's girl" embodies pure love and acceptance. Having a strong relationship with a father is important for girls, especially through those vulnerable adolescent years. How would you describe your relationship with your dad? Do any of your views of your dad get translated to how you view God? If so, how has this helped or hindered your experience of intimacy with God?

3. Life is full of lessons to be learned, lessons that reveal a great deal about our character. Being married provided opportunities to constantly learn things about how I operate and character issues I needed to change about myself, such as my habit of withholding love due to stubbornness. In what ways has marriage forced or helped you confront things you may need to change?

4. Relationships are significant to God. No matter how people treat Him, He continues to love extravagantly and unconditionally by offering the gift of His amazing grace to each of us. Are relationships significant to you? Do you have any relationships right now in which you need to extend grace and initiate reconciliation? In what ways can you do this?

CHAPTER 21
Depriving My Husband

In the midst of our sexless drought, Aaron confessed to me that he was still struggling with pornography. Unlike my noncommittal reaction before we were married, now I grew angry at him for not having self-control and for betraying my trust in that way. I already felt sexually inadequate, but the thought of him comparing me to the photos of "perfect" and always "available" women was devastating. I didn't see his addiction as one that had begun years prior to our relationship, which in fact it had. I was too blinded by hurt, thinking his addiction was a by-product of our unfulfilled marriage, that it was all my fault.

Oftentimes I would throw his struggle back at him, lashing out, raising my voice in disgust, purposefully trying to make him feel awful. I wasn't equipped to handle that kind of issue. I couldn't see the situation from my husband's perspective. I didn't even think of trying to understand how he was feeling about it. All I knew was the amount of pain it was inflicting on me. At one point I told him not to tell me about his struggle any longer—I didn't care that he was trying to apologize and allow me to keep him accountable. I thought if he needed to tell someone, he should have another man keep him accountable, because my frail heart could not bear his burden. I preferred to pretend it did not exist rather than face it.

Yet another moment of conviction would stir his heart to tell me when he struggled again.

No matter how much I expressed my hurt to my husband, he continued to fail me by secretly viewing pornography. I know he didn't do this intentionally to hurt me because he would often tell me that. He insisted it was because he had done it for so long that it was ingrained in his brain, but he also reassured me that he would try his hardest to fight against his desire for it. The fact that my husband wrestled with this sin tormented both of us. My Twilight obsession seemed to me to be nothing in comparison to the weight of shame imposed on our lives from his addiction, and I was growing weary of his inability to quit.

We found ourselves in a crazy cycle: his lust was superficially fulfilling his need for sexual release, while producing guilt in his heart, both of which ultimately altered his motivation to pursue me. His offense injured me in such a way that I rejected his affection, questioning whether he really wanted me or was driven only by his lust. Our intimacy was severed by sin. It took many fights, many nights of heartache and anguish, many conversations and prayers about this issue to get me to respond to my husband's weakness in a calm manner and for him to acknowledge the truth that he could be set free from his addiction. It took everything in me not to lash out when my husband told me when he messed up again, and I could only hope he was doing everything in his power to resist temptation. Whenever my husband told me that he'd viewed pornography, I had to turn to God and immediately hand over all my emotion and opinions to Him to prevent bitterness from building in my heart.

⊛   ⊛   ⊛

One night before Aaron jumped into the shower, he made an advance toward me. I quickly rejected his invitation to play, a common response on my part. I had become accustomed to going without, and my body didn't seem to mind. I shot him down with an unenthusiastic crinkle in my face that would surely deter anyone from bothering me. After a few minutes of the shower running, Aaron called my name. As I entered the bathroom, he whipped the shower curtain back and lifted both of his hands in the shape of a balancing scale.

With contempt in his voice he said, "You need to be careful when you reject me so often. I've been trying my hardest not to look at pornography." He glanced at one hand then the other hand, then back to me. "I can't have my wife. I need physical release, and I don't want to be tempted to look somewhere else."

I left the bathroom bothered by my husband's threat. I was furious at him for confronting the issue, that he had even mentioned his struggle with pornography, and that he was upset that I had said no to him. But even more, I was angry that I did not know how to improve our sex life. We had been grinding through three years of marriage, agonizing over our sexless life together. We had only experienced a handful of mediocre moments of sexual intimacy, nothing truly satisfying for either of us. The pain that I experienced during intercourse was still affecting me, and I hated anticipating that pain or the time it took to get anywhere. My mind was battered, my body was broken, and my heart was over it all. I had given up. I had nothing left to help me endure as hopelessness carved from my heart the once-strong desire for my husband.

I suppose the numbness I felt was localized and I accepted the conclusion that I didn't need him to fulfill me sexually, so I shut down that part of me. However, avoiding sex resulted in catastrophe. I was depriving my husband of whatever intimacy I was able to give him, which bruised his heart every time I said no.

Aaron's words sank in my soul like an anchor. The image of his hands as scales weighing everything in the balance stuck with me. I knew that he wasn't so much threatening to look elsewhere; rather, my husband was sending a clear message that I was withholding from him, leaving him with an ultimate no, which meant his needs would never be met—at least in a God-honoring way.

Up to this point, instead of complaining about the way I rejected him, Aaron allowed himself to succumb to the porn temptation, searching to be fulfilled even in a counterfeit way. But recently God had been moving in his life to rid him of his desire for pornography, retraining the way he had been wired. So now that he was refusing pornography as an option, he was at a wall. Every time he received a no from me, his needs went unmet and he had to go without, since he had nowhere else *to* go. Just because I was able to shut down sexually didn't mean he could. And it certainly didn't mean he should!

Whether I wanted to acknowledge it or not, *both* of our bodies were designed with a need for sexual release. As much as it hurt me to hear my husband accuse me of rejecting him, that is what I was doing. My husband's addiction to pornography was his struggle, but when I rejected him, it pushed him further into the embracing arms of counterfeit intimacy. I desired my husband to be set free from the bondage of his addiction, and he was making incredible strides to overcome as God transformed that part of him, but I became a stumbling block because I would not fulfill his needs.

The day when my husband communicated that truth to me, once I calmed down, God helped me comprehend the gravity of this issue. His holy words caught my attention and challenged me to change.

> Do not deprive each other of sexual relations, unless you both agree to refrain from sexual intimacy for a limited time so you can give yourselves more completely to prayer. Afterward, you should come together again so that Satan won't be able to tempt you because of your lack of self-control.
>
> I CORINTHIANS 7:5

I knew we needed to reconcile and it was my move. Initiating in our relationship was always a challenge for me. I didn't know how to climb over the wall in my heart that seemed so insurmountable and join my husband. I could sense my feet starting to itch as a craving to run in the opposite direction sprang up.

With the exhaustion of our full-time jobs, our work on the weekends as professional photographers, and the fact that we were still living with my mom and stepdad, I asked Aaron to hold on. We were preparing for an upcoming trip to Maui, where we were scheduled to photograph a wedding, but we'd have a whole week after the ceremony to explore the exotic island. I begged him to use that vacation time to reignite our intimacy, convinced that making up for our honeymoon with a trip to Hawaii would be the cure, and the perfect time to work on romance.

I was once again searching for that new experience or atmosphere to bring change to our circumstance—yet another escape. While looking forward to this new adventure was invigorating, I was ashamed to consider that I still hadn't learned my lesson.

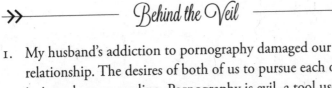

Behind the Veil

1. My husband's addiction to pornography damaged our relationship. The desires of both of us to pursue each other intimately were eroding. Pornography is evil, a tool used by the enemy to destroy people's lives. Has your life been affected by pornography? Has your husband been honest with you about struggling with it? If so, how did that information affect you and your relationship with him?

2. So many negative emotions are born in a sin such as pornography, including inadequacy, insecurity, shame, and guilt. When these emotions start to swirl, it becomes easier for bitterness and resentment to settle in as well. What are some sins that you or your husband have struggled with? What emotions have been stirred up by those sins?

CHAPTER 22

Inception

Giving Aaron hope that I would work on our romance was easier said than done. We were still looking forward to Maui, but as I relied on that trip to be our time of change, I neglected to focus on how I could fulfill his needs in the meantime. I excused myself from making any effort to draw close to him.

As my stress grew from our everyday challenges, I began to have vivid dreams. One night I dreamed that another man met up with me, a man who was not my husband. Although my dream was fuzzy and did not make much sense, I developed strong feelings for this man, a friend from my past. In my dream I was flirting with him, and he was reciprocating the interest. For the first time in a long time, I felt beautiful, wanted, worthy. When I woke up, I could not stop thinking about him and the way he had made me feel. I glanced over at my husband lying asleep next to me and felt guilty that I wanted to dwell on this other man. It felt weird to be attracted to someone other than my husband. Although I'd fantasized about the Twilight fiction, this was different. This man was real. I knew embracing those feelings was wrong, but it also made me feel alive. Confusion and doubt took jabs at me with questions about why my husband had not been able to make me feel this way in a long time.

After a few days of constantly replaying the dream, I casually suggested to Aaron that we should hang out with this friend. In such a short time my infatuation, sprouted from my dream, had become an obsession. I daydreamed about being with this other man, thinking how life would be better if I divorced Aaron to be with him or someone like him.

I was no longer satisfied with simply reliving the dream, I felt the urge, the craving for more—I desired to see him in person. But that came with a price: entertaining such thoughts led me to further isolate myself from Aaron. Any progress we may have made was crushed by my new crush. I couldn't stop thinking about this guy, and every day I drew closer to convincing myself that I should leave Aaron.

Before, when I'd fleetingly considered divorce, I'd always dismissed it, remembering my pledge never to experience what my parents had. This time things changed. Now when the thought of divorce popped into my mind, I allowed it to linger. I entertained more seriously how much better my life would be without Aaron in it.

❀   ❀   ❀

My spirit fought against my flesh in a messy war. I knew I was sinning against Aaron, even though I had not acted on the things I was contemplating. Jesus' words in Matthew 5:27-28 pricked my heart: "You have heard the commandment that says, 'You must not commit adultery.' But I say, anyone who even looks at a woman with lust has already committed adultery with her in his heart."

Apathy had set in again in my tug-of-war relationship with God, and I pushed each word away in denial. I knew the difference between right and wrong, and I knew the stark contrast between God's truth and the enemy's lies, yet I chose to welcome the latter with an open heart. I often told myself, *What difference does it make, really? My marriage is failing anyway. It's my turn to be happy, and I should do anything to get it.* Despite my flesh falling for this deception, my spirit saw it for what it was: evil. A huge contributor to the sin I allowed into my life was believing that my happiness was a priority and that I should do everything in my ability to chase after it. As God was trying to move in our marriage, I drove Him away, allowing the enemy to jump in and stop any progress we experienced. The enemy took advantage of me when I was weak, and the worst part was that I let him.

Although I never told Aaron how strong my feelings were about leaving him and potentially finding someone else, my attitude surely gave it away. I turned bitter cold toward Aaron, more than ever before. I intentionally built a wall of separation between us. From my side of the wall, I reasoned that if I changed just enough and became undesirable, Aaron would leave me on his own, releasing me of fault. I put him down in front of others, I annoyed him, I snapped at him, and I tried to pick fights with him, all on purpose. The truth was that I wanted him to hate me as much as I hated myself. I believed that was what I deserved.

⊛　　⊛　　⊛

One Wednesday night, feeling particularly perturbed about attending the marriage group, I got into the car and forcibly slammed the door. I was fed up with my husband and his desire to keep going to the sessions. Marriage was too much for me to handle. That door slam and my frustration, which I expressed through crossed arms and a sour face, was another way I tried to manipulate Aaron into hating our marriage too. To drive it home, I inquired for the third time if we were going to make plans to visit my friend.

"Why are you all of a sudden so interested in getting together with this guy?"

He saw through me as if I were made of glass, and I broke. I confessed how everything had snowballed from the dream I had a week earlier. With a contrite spirit, I tried to explain the emotional effects of all that was happening, including the defeat I felt in our relationship. Astonishingly, my husband did not express anger or even disappointment, although I knew it was impossible for him not to experience those things. He held back his emotion with dignity and he forgave me. He said he was not going to give up on us and he hoped that I wouldn't either.

In that moment of transparency, embarrassment, and shame, I experienced the amazing gift of grace, an offering my husband was able to extend to me only because of the beautiful gift of grace he received from God. I realized I had been walking in darkness, under the facade of following God. My sin came to light along with the ramifications that I had the potential to destroy my marriage. I was faced with a decision: Do I continue to do things my way, which had resulted in a dwindled faith and broken marriage? Or do I surrender—really surrender—to God in humility with a heart of repentance and accept God's discipline as a means to refinement?

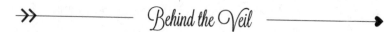

Behind the Veil

1. My desperation to feel wholly satisfied propelled my acceptance for things I had once strongly believed were outside my character. I craved something deeper, something emotionally recharging: I craved true intimacy. In my despair I searched for that "something" in the wrong way. On my path to destruction, God used my husband to stop me in my tracks, but I had to choose to expose the truth that really snapped me out of it! In times that you feel despair or dissatisfaction, do you dwell on things that are outside your character or against God's will? How does the enemy take advantage of your weakness to turn you against your husband?

2. The allure of happiness is bait the enemy uses to take our eyes off Jesus and off our spouse. In what ways have you been lured by elusive happiness? What was the result? Why is joy more powerful and righteous than happiness?

3. I received abundant grace in the midst of my sin. I am incredibly thankful that God helped the truth come to light so that I did not continue down a path of unrighteousness. In less than a week I experienced deep shame, then extraordinary forgiveness, then overwhelming peace. If you have been or are in this hard place now, and are thinking negative thoughts or pushing your husband away, think about the root cause of what is motivating you to do such things. What can you do to change these negative patterns you have fallen into?

CHAPTER 23

Transparency

"Aaron, can we talk?" I found my husband lying in bed, ready to go to sleep.

Three and a half years of turmoil was too much of a burden for me to carry any longer. The honeymoon had been over for a while; it was time to unpack . . . everything. That night I thought again about the dream I'd had a few weeks back, my obsession with desiring another man, and Aaron's pornography confession, and God pressed upon me to be completely honest with my husband. The countless nights spent around a table filled with married couples sharing their stories had shown me the power of transparency. My heart was encouraged to be just as brave.

I spent a lot of time praying about my struggle and knew it was time now to talk with Aaron about it. My heart was pounding in my chest and my palms were sweaty.

"I am really sorry for what happened a few weeks ago. I feel awful that I allowed myself to think about being with any man other than you. It started all because of a dream that I had, and because we've been struggling. I was weak, and I acknowledge I sinned against God and you. I'm so sorry for hurting you like that, and I want you to know that I really want us to work out our problems. My desire is that God gives us a miracle and transforms our marriage. I love you, Aaron."

"I forgive you. I want us to work it out too." I could feel Aaron's grace in those heartfelt words.

I tried to explain how the hardships coming against our marriage were affecting me. I felt it was important to address how each issue we encountered was exponentially adding up, ultimately feeding my depression.

I exposed parts of my heart that I had never shared before, not with anyone. I stuttered through my words, hoping and praying Aaron would continue to receive them with grace. I told my husband how our inability to have sex forced me to question and sometimes doubt the love we shared. And then I paused, more painfully aware of my next confession. I struggled to look at Aaron as I told him that during the times we attempted sex, it was difficult for me to get aroused. And though it may have been from anticipating that I would experience physical pain, I also began to wonder if maybe I was not attracted to my husband for a specific reason: that perhaps I was attracted to women.

I could feel my face flush as I confessed such an idea. I didn't want to think about the possibility of being a lesbian. I knew it contradicted my faith in God, His divine design, and His Word. I felt conflicted and ashamed about even considering such a thing. I told myself that it would damage my husband's spirit if I told him I was struggling in my sexuality amid our own sexual challenges. Yet I also recognized that the longer I kept it buried, the more I seemed to be tormented.

I opened up to my husband, unsure if he would accept the real me, the imperfect me. My soul peered through the torn edges of the veil that had once protected me—or so I thought. I wanted to throw it back over my head and hide, but tonight was different. God helped me to remove the barrier that had separated my husband and me for so long. A transparent river of truth, emotion, and uncertainty flowed from me, sentence after sentence.

I continued to reveal to Aaron my truest nature, explaining that questioning my sexuality came around the same time I began looking at pornography a year and a half into our marriage.

His jaw dropped.

In that moment I thought about all the times Aaron had been honest with me about his pornography addiction. He let me know when times were difficult, and we prayed through it together, but even so, he struggled to kick the horrible habit.

I knew that during our sex drought he leaned more toward pornography than ever before to fulfill his sexual needs, which had been a huge contribution to why he stopped pursuing me romantically. Although he tried telling me when times were more tempting, or when he apologized out of shame, I often pushed him away. I knew his addiction existed before our marriage, but I felt responsible for his need to be fulfilled elsewhere because I was *unavailable*. But the truth was that I also responded out of guilt from my own secret sins, desiring that they remain hidden. And that secret created a chasm between us that I wanted to pretend did not exist. Knowing he was being tempted with pornography caused a deep pain of insecurity in my heart, but it also fueled *my* curiosity.

❀   ❀   ❀

I had been exposed to pornography when I was younger, and with easy access to the Internet I knew where to seek it. I did not understand when or how it gained such a rule over my life; just like my husband, I became a slave to my own lust. I understood the weight of my husband's addiction all too well, even though I never wanted to tell him. I felt like confessing such a sin would somehow condone his actions or make them less hurtful toward me. I was deceived, but unlike Aaron, I was left without any accountability to help me defend my heart or marriage against such evil.

When a craving to look at explicit images manifested itself, I stumbled through thousands of different photos, the majority of which included females. I fantasized about being those women. A desire to be sexy, to feel wanted, to experience a good sexual encounter, all pulled me into a world of lust where I tried to create an environment or circumstance that fulfilled me. I was filling my mind with these images, unknowingly connecting sexual gratification with females, which fed an intensely growing craving.

Looking at such graphic images stains the mind, but I didn't care about the consequences. I just wanted something to fill the void. I had recently learned from the book Joanne gave me that a biological process happens in the human body through sexual stimulation, and an unhealthy habit that triggers such a process, such as pornography, is a recipe for destruction of marital oneness. Our lack of gratification with each other was being fulfilled elsewhere and the secrecy was killing our marriage.

⊛　　⊛　　⊛

Aaron locked eyes with me. His face was full of concern and worry. There was also a hint of sadness. Although I could tell he seemed eager to hear me finish, he interrupted me.

"Babe, I am so sorry you've had to deal with this."

Taking in a deep breath, I wiped my wet cheeks with my sleeve and then exhaled what was left inside me. During our conversation I saw a glimpse of how deception weaves its way through life, suffocating the beauty of truth that God created.

It became obvious that the only reason I had been questioning my sexuality was because of the sin I'd allowed to infiltrate my heart. As I realized how the unhealthy connections I was making through willfully using pornography to self-stimulate was affecting my body chemistry, confusing the very design God established, I no longer believed I might be a lesbian. My sin was blinding me from seeing things clearly, but as God unveiled the truth, I gained an understanding of what was really happening. My flesh was being satisfied even though it was not in the way God intended, and I believe the enemy used my disobedience as an opportunity to oppress me by tempting me with the desire to lust for more. With each decision I made to look at another explicit image or video, I was training my body to walk down a path that led me away from God, away from my husband, and even away from the woman I was purposed to be.

I was terrified of being judged or humiliated for so long that I'd told myself I must deal with this embarrassing struggle on my own. I was also hesitant to expose my struggle because women's addiction to pornography is rarely talked about, especially in Christian environments. I didn't want to be the one labeled and defined by my sin. For years, the same lie ran through my mind: *I'm the only one, and others would never understand, not even my husband.* However, as God was refining me and teaching me about my different issues, it became evident that I was not going to be able to overcome this without accountability. I also perceived that it would remain a source of contention in our marriage unless, with God's strength, I exposed the truth.

I believe God anointed my conversation with my husband that night. A sense of relief washed over me. Peace covered me like a blanket, comforting me in my most vulnerable moment. My husband listened intently to all I revealed to him, responding gently and respectfully. He scooted closer toward me on the bed and wrapped his arms around me.

With his head pressed against mine, he said, "I know that wasn't easy to share with me, but I appreciate you telling me. And I am positive you are not the only one who struggles with understanding your sexuality, especially when we are challenged with things like pornography."

His response made me feel more normal, but even so, I realized that if I could so easily get entangled in pornography and confused about my sexuality, there was no telling how many other women were really struggling with it—including Christians who deeply love the Lord and want to have good marriages. I wondered who else was discovering the depths of consequences to such sin. My husband and I held each other tightly and prayed over our lives, our marriage, and the various threats that come against us.

We stayed up late into the night talking through our personal struggles, perceptions, and doubts, as well as confronting those that affected our marriage. The more transparent we were with each other, the more we were encouraged to share, exchanging forgiveness and grace for our past behaviors. We gained an understanding of each other that night and an invaluable appreciation for transparency. Our connection brought us to a place of intimacy we had never experienced before as a couple. We were making ourselves truly known to each other. I was grateful for the Holy Spirit's conviction—and I was thankful I had finally obeyed and confessed my struggles.

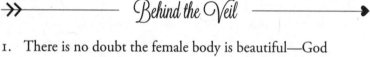

Behind the Veil

1. There is no doubt the female body is beautiful—God created it to be—but when perversity masquerades itself beneath a banner of acceptability, the female body becomes a token of lust and infatuation, an idol. I knew pornography was a sin, but I never fully understood the harm I was doing to my mind or my marriage. Sometimes emotional pain can lead to such destructive apathy. Have you knowingly sinned, disregarding the potential consequences? If so, what were some of those consequences? How do you think differently now?

2. I believe the enemy used my husband's addiction to pornography as a weakness in our marriage to also tempt me, by luring me into it with curiosity of what captivated him. In what ways do you think you have sinned because of the weak areas in which your husband sins? In what

ways do you think the enemy has lured your husband to sin because of your weaknesses?

3. Unveiling myself to my husband was terrifying and risky because I wasn't sure he would respond to me with grace. What are some reasons you withhold feelings or thoughts from your husband? Why do you think unveiling yourself to your husband could help you? What things would you want to tell him?

CHAPTER 24

Standing for Marriage

The next Sunday at church we felt God pursuing us passionately. The entire sermon was specifically tailored to the topic of pornography. Minutes into our pastor's message, I began to feel uneasy. Even though I had confessed my sin to my husband, the guilt and shame from things that I had done still infested my heart. While I was sitting in the service, God brought John 15:1-2 to mind, a verse my husband had recently been reciting and trying to memorize:

> I am the true vine, and my Father is the gardener. He cuts off every branch in me that bears no fruit, while every branch that does bear fruit he prunes so that it will be even more fruitful. (NIV)

As I thought about those verses, I began to understand that God was pruning the parts of my character that were unrighteous and grafting me into His pure vine. He wanted me there that morning, listening to a brave sermon about the effects of pornography right after I had just confessed such sin to my husband. God was reinforcing in me and affirming that He was present and near. God was walking us through this, all the while using what we encountered to transform us.

Midway through the message, our pastor mentioned how women are also tempted by pornography, something I had never heard spoken in the church. He continued to point out more specifically the negative effects pornography has on marriages, such as hindering intimacy, skewing expectations of sex, and destroying trust.

The content was striking and extremely relevant to us. I placed my head on Aaron's shoulder, trying to hide my teary eyes from others sitting close to us. Every word struck a chord in my heart. Certain that I was beet red and covered in melted makeup, I wanted to get up and leave, but I was trapped. I was afraid people would see me crying and question me. Although I was willing to divulge my sin to my husband, I was *not* prepared to let another person know the extent of who I really was. Besides, I was pinned in the middle section of a large row of people, some of whom were our friends.

The weight of my burden and my yearning to experience freedom were overwhelming. I wept silently and tried to inconspicuously wipe my wet face. At the end of the sermon the pastor invited anyone forward who was eager to receive freedom from pornography and healing in their marriage.

My husband squeezed my hand. I didn't want to acknowledge the steps God was offering us to reconcile our hearts. I knew that if we walked forward, people, including our friends, would be aware of our struggle. It was too hard to humble myself enough to let others know that my character was full of faults. My sleeve was soaked with tears and snot. I was sure I had mascara running down my puffy cheeks.

My husband squeezed my hand again. I looked up to catch just as much emotion swirling in his eyes. This was hard for him, too, but I realized that he cared more about our relationship than other people's judgments.

Wiping my face, I nodded, and Aaron and I walked toward the front of the church. We stood with countless others who'd gathered the courage, embraced the humility, and made the walk. Our pastor prayed over us. Then he encouraged us to speak with a decision counselor, a volunteer at the church to help us process the decision we'd made regarding why we were moved to go forward.

❈   ❈   ❈

We entered the side room for counseling and saw Chris and Joanne follow us.

Chris put his hand on Aaron's shoulder. "Can we talk with you guys about going forward?"

I nodded and looked at Aaron to make sure we were on the same page, and he also nodded. We sat together, and once again, God gave me the courage to express how I was feeling, pushing me to reveal what I had been struggling with. I cried as I explained to Chris and Joanne what I had shared with my husband. My heart pounded wildly, but I got through it. When I finished, Aaron shared his point of view.

Chris and Joanne looked at us with such forgiving eyes. Their compassion overwhelmed me in a perfect and holy way. Then they prayed with us. Aaron and I recommitted our lives to each other and to the pursuit of having a fulfilled marriage. We were sure that the emotional experience would help us stay true to each other and give us the strength to fight pornography's temptation as a team.

After that Sunday, our marriage began to improve dramatically. We were devoted to making ourselves known to God and known to each other. I finally felt free from the bondage that was holding me captive. I could breathe deeply without fear of someone finding out who I was, because I had chosen to make myself known. I felt like a whole new woman.

Hopefulness for where our marriage was headed reignited my desire for Aaron. We dug into the Bible more consistently, seeking after truth and wanting a more intimate relationship with God. We also sought after each other. We made more of an effort to pursue each other by going on dates and becoming aware of each other's needs. We attempted to enjoy sexual intimacy without being hindered while sex was not an option.

I was learning that having a strong marital foundation is important, but it requires investment. And I was learning that strong relational foundations are built by experiences of trust. My investment as a wife involves cultivating trust in my marriage—a safe place where I can be honest with my husband and he can be honest with me. The more Aaron and I were able to be transparent with each other, the more I began to trust our relationship. Being open and honest with my husband about what I was going through was vital because in those moments of raw vulnerability, he came to know the real me.

Likewise, when my husband was open and honest with me, I learned to be controlled in my response, led by the Holy Spirit. If I punished my husband or quickly reacted from being hurt—all responses I had used previously—that only caused him to push away and avoid being transparent with me. I discovered that the key to cultivating trust when my husband and I are being transparent with each other is to give each other the room to open up in a conversation, both taking turns listening and talking, while agreeing that no matter what we say, the desired result is reconciliation. But the most important thing I discovered was that I was only truly able to be transparent when God helped me through each and every moment. I simply couldn't do it on my own.

>> ———— *Behind the Veil* ————>

1. Although a few times after that moment of recognition and repentance we still met failure, we did not stay pressed down by shame. We were determined to rid ourselves of impurity, and we were faithfully confident it was possible because we were submitting to God. My husband and I kept each

other accountable by giving permission to inquire about the progress we were making. Do you and your husband keep each other accountable to righteous living? How will keeping each other accountable contribute to a better marriage?

2. I learned that if I refused to communicate to my husband or if I made it difficult for him to approach me, we would never experience deep intimacy and we would never provide the opportunity to build trust with each other. Likewise, if you resist being unveiled *and* if you do not allow your husband the freedom to be transparent, you will not provide the opportunity for trust to thrive in your marriage. What are three things you can do to become unveiled? What are three things you can do to provide a safe environment for your husband to be unveiled before you?

3. Reconciliation is an important aspect of marriage. Husbands and wives constantly need to apologize and forgive because we are all sinners and fail each other daily. To be able to pursue reconciliation in your marriage, you must first pursue reconciliation with God. He has already provided the way to reconciliation through His Son, Jesus Christ, so by believing in Him and receiving Him as your Savior, you enter into a relationship with God. An intimate relationship with God comes when you offer yourself fully to Him, make yourself known to Him, and reciprocate affection by loving Him. Do you and God have an intimate relationship? What do you still need to address in your relationship with God to make yourself fully known to Him? What outstanding issues do you need to reconcile with your husband?

4. When I began to understand how my relationship with God dramatically affects who I am as a wife, I really contemplated how intimacy with God overflows into having intimacy

CHAPTER 25
The Getaway

M aui was breathtaking. The sky and the water were magnificent shades of blue. The air was crisp and clear. Palm trees danced in the breeze without any encumbrance, and the warm air whipped around us as we soaked up the new landscape. The first few days of our trip were busy preparing for the wedding we would be photographing. After the wedding, we would be free to experience a honeymoon of our own—we had still been trying to make up for the original trip we'd taken almost four years prior.

A storm hit the island early in the morning the day of the ceremony. We worried the rain would ruin the special day, but on our way to breakfast, as we walked down the main street in town, the sun broke through the clouds and the sky cleared up. Aaron and I went to a café on Front Street and sat at a small round table for two. Giant windows with white shutters hung wide open beside us providing a beautiful view of the ocean. I thought about our wedding day and the joy I'd had about becoming a wife. So much had changed me since saying "I do," and I wondered if this was how God wanted our story to play out.

That hour with Aaron over breakfast inspired me to capture the love expressed throughout the wedding. The ceremony was romantic and profound as our friends made a covenant of marriage. Seeing their joy and love for each other once again reminded me of the joy we had on our wedding day. I wanted to reconnect with Aaron and work toward fulfilling the joy we experienced during our special day.

⊛   ⊛   ⊛

Finally with the wedding in our rearview mirror, we deserted any desires to plan, heading out instead to spontaneously explore the island. We drove up and down every road we found; we got ourselves lost in a coffee plantation; we sat on the warm sandy beach; and we swam right next to massive sea turtles. We ate delicious food, we snorkeled in search of tropical fish, we saw the sunrise from the peak of Haleakala, and we even ventured out on the Road to Hana. The scenery was majestic. We savored flavored shaved ice, fish tacos, nightly strolls, and an entertaining luau. We had the time of our lives discovering Maui.

But again, amid the joy we found on the island, our hearts were stressed with the weight of a familiar feeling. Every day we were there we had copious time to relish in physical intimacy with each other. Aaron insisted from the beginning that we not rush into trying to have sex, but take each day as it comes, worried that I might psyche myself into a fit of anxiety. Yet no matter how gently we eased our way into the situation, pain still inflamed my body. We had convinced ourselves we would make it work while we were in Maui, that the magic of the island would throw us into a romantic environment that would stimulate us the right way. And we prayed in faith that God would grant us a miracle. Unfortunately, we did not see the fruits of our prayers. I could not believe a week of adventures on the island came and went. And on Saturday, our final day, as we headed to the airport, I struggled with mixed emotions, grateful for the memories we'd made and bitter for the ones we didn't.

⊛ ⊛ ⊛

The weeks following our trip were depressing. Instead of talking about it, however, I sank back into isolation, watching helplessly as we wandered further apart. For some reason, it was hard to address how I was feeling. I know I was unhappy because I felt at fault for our lack of intercourse and could not bring myself to talk about it anymore. The anticipation of Maui being a time of healing and restoration was shattered, leaving me wounded. With sadness pressing me down, my responses toward Aaron again became short, snappy, and selfish. I could not resolve the lack of intimacy that burdened our marriage, and my inability to understand or find an answer to *Why us?* fueled my frustrations.

I assumed Aaron was just as frustrated. Although we had made some incredible progress, especially maturing in our ability to communicate with each other, I began turning hard again, my soul stone cold, my mind trapped beneath the weight of it all, and my body barely able to compose itself. I was beyond pathetic and wasting away, each day growing closer to misery as Aaron and I drifted apart.

Shortly after our trip to Maui, my love for Aaron was challenged. We drove down the highway in silence, yet the tension between us was thick. We were on our way to a photography job we had scheduled almost a year before, an obligation we could not back out of. I was full of contempt for my husband as I struggled with feeling unloved. I kept reminding myself of *my* needs, resulting in a maddening and ice-frosted attitude toward Aaron, which in turn irritated him even more. I never stopped to understand how he was feeling and why.

Once we were there and set up, though, everything just seemed to get worse, if that were possible. Glancing toward Aaron to see if he was ready to take pictures, my heart sank with grief. He looked so solemn. His eyes drooped as if he was checked out in his mind.

"Are you okay?"

He shook his head. And his look said, *I don't want to talk about it.*

I didn't know what else to do, and I was frustrated that he would not respond to me.

"Well, you need to smile and pretend to be fine or else go sit in the car!" My approach was stern, but all I could think of was that we were minutes away from photographing an event, and I needed my partner to snap out of it. I put our relationship aside for business, and although my cold heart was able to say what I said, something inside me knew it was wrong. Instead of questioning my priorities, I put work first without hesitation, forcing my husband to join me.

He nodded grimly. "I'll try."

I went back to my spot and prepared to start shooting.

A few more hours passed before we could call it a night. My husband, usually so constant—like a rock, strong enough to brush off any pressures that came against him or our relationship— proved to be something else. By the time we got home, I was exhausted, and Aaron didn't seem to have it in him to share his burden at all. We both seemed to have finally reached our limit.

⟫ ———— Behind the Veil ————➤

1. I expected our getaway to Maui to be exactly what we needed to solve our greatest struggle. I thought being on an exotic island would stimulate our relationship and help us connect deeper than we ever had before. But when those expectations went unfulfilled, disappointment overwhelmed me. Has there been a time when you hoped a getaway would solve your problems? If you and your husband went on that trip, what resulted? If you strongly feel a getaway for a while will help, why do you feel that way?

2. Life is constantly full of good times and challenging ones. Amid our disappointment on the island, we had the

opportunity to explore and experience an amazing new place. I believe it is important to note the ways my husband and I enjoy life together despite our problems, to remind me that married life may not be perfectly good all the time, but when it is, it is really good. What adventures have you and your husband shared? Have any of those good experiences been during difficult seasons?

3. As Aaron and I worked together, it became obvious that something was terribly wrong with him. I cared more about what people thought and about our commitment to the job than I cared about his emotional breakdown. I also didn't know how to help my husband, and that insecurity motivated me to snap at him, hoping it would resuscitate him. I failed to consider the one thing that might have actually done that: I neglected to pray for him. How often do you rush past opportunities to pray for your husband or show him how much you care? Do obligations, such as work, ever motivate you to snap at your husband? Why is doing that dangerous for marriage?

CHAPTER 26

Unconditional Love

W e woke the next morning and went to church. It was obvious Aaron was still upset. He barely said one word to me the entire morning, and his eyes drooped in sadness. I had never seen him so dismal, and I wasn't sure how to approach him. The drive to church was quiet and emotionally cold. I did what was familiar to me and slapped on a smile, hoping it would stick long enough to get me through the morning. We sat next to a few friends, and as I listened to the sermon my eyes kept wandering toward Aaron. His head hung down for most of the service, a posture of absolute defeat.

I knew we'd reached the end. I couldn't keep up this relationship the way it was, and I was sure he couldn't either. Still, though, I feared talking about divorce, an inevitable fate for two people who could not satisfy each other. We were suffocating beneath the weight of despair.

Can no one see it but me?

⊕   ⊕   ⊕

When the service concluded, I followed Aaron out of the row of chairs where he stopped and asked our friend Tom if he had time to talk. Tom had invited us to sit at his table our first night at the married community group we attended. He and his wife had become our trusted best friends. Tom agreed and he, his wife, and I followed Aaron to a quiet spot in the sanctuary.

Aaron began sharing how upset he was, tormented that our sex life had never been fulfilling. I was not expecting him to open up like this, and I felt hurt and ashamed as I heard the deep pain in his tone, but I simply listened. There was nothing I could say to defend myself.

Aaron looked back and forth between Tom and me as he said, "I think we both had placed high expectations on Maui being a solution to our problem. But ever since we've been back, I haven't been able to shake the disappointment."

I was so familiar with failing expectations in our sex life that I had become calloused, while Aaron had always been so patient. Now it was clear he was unable to withstand the encumbrance any longer. Tears welled up in his eyes as he expressed how much pain he had endured over the years—from the unmet anticipation of a satisfying marriage all the way to this point.

He wiped tears from his eyes. "Lately I've just been feeling like I'm at the end of my rope. Every time I look at my wife I want to have a great marriage, but I'm reminded of the areas we struggle with and can't seem to overcome. I have never been so depressed. Ask Jennifer. I know the last few days she has seen a difference in me."

In that moment I witnessed a solid man falter beneath the weight of an emotional and physical burden he had been carrying for almost four years. I could see that he, like me, desperately desired a marriage fulfilled in every way, and he didn't understand why God would not move in mighty ways to help us. It was hard to witness my husband so wrecked. He stood there releasing pent up frustration, anger, and pain. I grew ashamed again as I realized how selfless my husband had been this whole time—and how selfish I had been. I never knew. I drew my hand to my lip, a nervous thing I did when I felt a rush of emotion hit me.

Aaron inhaled deeply. "Today as I was sitting in church stewing in frustration over my marriage, I felt God give me an epiphany. I saw a vision of Jesus praying in the garden of Gethsemane. Jesus, knowing fully what He was about to endure, asked God to let the cup pass from His lips. Jesus was looking for an escape so that He did not have to bear being separated from His Father. He asked God three times for the cup to be taken and three times that God's will be done. Jesus' prayer reveals the battle between His flesh and His Spirit. Regardless of what would happen to His flesh, He ultimately desired God's will. Jesus understood that God needed Him to be the sacrifice for everyone. God's love for people motivated Jesus' love to be the atoning sacrifice. That kind of love is powerful."

Aaron stopped abruptly and blinked hard. "Sorry, I am just overwhelmed by the fact God just showed me, that true love will always sacrifice for the sake of others. Just as Jesus laid down His life for the church—God's people—so a husband is to lay down his life for his bride. I am supposed to lay down my life for my wife."

As I listened to Aaron's passionate speech and revelation, I stood in awe of the powerful correlation God had revealed to him.

In front of our friend Tom and his wife, who wept alongside us, Aaron lifted his hands and firmly held my cheeks, forcing me to look him in the eyes as he apologized.

"I am so sorry for getting frustrated because our sex life has not been satisfying. I commit to continuing our pursuit to find a solution, but more than that I promise to truly love you no matter what the outcome is. In the last four years we've learned how to be intimate without sex, we have grown in our relationship despite the pain of feeling unfulfilled, we have found creative ways to love each other, and we've discovered other needs that we had as a husband and wife, some that were direct results of not having sex and many others that could be met without it."

I tilted my head down to wipe a few tears, but with Aaron's hands still cupping my face, he lifted my head back up and continued to assure me with the most romantic words anyone has ever said to me, "I will always be faithful to you, I will start intentionally pursuing you again, and I will strive to love you as Jesus loves us."

My husband pulled me close, kissed my forehead, and held me in a tight hug. I felt a rush of God's peace over both of us, along with many more tears that had been held back by the resentment of feeling unfulfilled in our relationship. My walls were still coming down. We stood humbly before each other and our friends, committing to stand and fight for our marriage! We left church that day with a renewed spirit, a willingness to keep investing love into our marriage, and a faith in each other that we would grow old together, no matter what may come!

The revelation my husband shared with me was a significant reminder of what it truly means to love. Christ is the perfect example of unconditional, sacrificial, serving love. Christ knew what God needed Him to do, and the anguish gripped His heart so much that He wept and He sweat blood (Luke 22:44).

The agony He endured was much more than the physical abuse He was prepared to bear. The Bible does not go into detail about all the thoughts running through Jesus' mind in that moment in the garden of Gethsemane, the night before He was crucified, but I wonder if He thought of all the people He was about to suffer for who would reject His love. I wonder if He thought about the people who would never experience just how much love He had for them. I wonder if He thought about those who would choose not to receive His amazing grace. I believe Christ's compassion stirred grief and heartache knowing He was motivated by a love that would not be reciprocated by all. Yet He did it anyway.

How could I truly love my husband if I did not assume that same posture? To serve him, to sacrifice for him, to lay down my selfishness and live wholeheartedly to point him toward the awesome sovereignty of God, just as Jesus does for me.

It was amazing to me that instead of talking about the end of our relationship, Aaron spoke so beautifully of God's message to him, which allowed us to focus on the future of our marriage. We were on the edge of what could have been our greatest mistake, yet God had other plans.

>>───────── *Behind the Veil* ─────────→

1. God helped me readjust my focus once again by showing me the character of Christ and the example He set for me. He was thinking of me when He went to the cross, with joy set before Him, a holy act of self-abandonment (Hebrews 12:2). He did it for me, fully knowing how often I would reject Him. Christ is also an example for you. His desire has always been to show you true love. He also desires that you exude the same character and reflect the gospel of redemption in the way you love your husband. In what ways can striving to love like Christ positively affect your marriage? How is loving your husband unconditionally a reflection to others of the gospel?

2. I tried to hold back tears as I heard my husband open up about how he felt and what God was teaching him. Then when Aaron turned to me and poured out his heart while holding me, I melted and so did the hardships that seemed to be mounting. That kind of vulnerability is powerful. Has your husband ever been vulnerable in communicating how he feels toward you? How does it impact you? If he hasn't, would you pray intentionally and ask God to motivate your husband's heart to do so?

3. God kept our marriage from falling apart that day. His holy perspective enlightened my husband's heart, and in turn my heart for our future together. God reconciled us through the powerful love story of Christ's unconditional love for people. In what ways has the gospel impacted your marriage and the way you and your husband love each other? In what ways has God helped you stand for your marriage?

CHAPTER 27

Our Miracle

J ust a few days after the emotional episode at church, Aaron
and I stumbled onto an interesting discovery, prompted by his
pursuit to improve our sex life. While taking a shower, Aaron
called my name. My heart sank with worry. I had seen this situation play out before—and it never ended well.

"Jennifer!" he yelled again, this time more urgently.

"Yeah?" I said, now more curious than worried.

"Remember when Joanne was talking about her friend who
switched out her products and got pregnant?"

"I remember." I walked into the bathroom to hear him better.
"What about it?"

"What if there was something in the environment causing your
body not to work the way it's supposed to?" Aaron flung back part
of the curtain and popped his head out to complete his thought.
"What is the only product you have used for the last six years?"

"My face wash, I think."

"Yes! Everything else you have switched and changed numerous times, but you have used this—" he held out my facial wash
bottle, "consistently—what, once a day? Twice a day?"

"Exactly. I use it a lot because I need it." I figured out where
he was going with his line of reasoning and wasn't interested at

all. "No, Aaron. Sorry, but I can't stop using my face wash!" I'd suffered from acne through most of my adolescence, and the only thing that had worked was that facial wash. I walked out of the bathroom and sat on our bed.

Aaron did not hesitate to jump out of the shower and get dressed. He grabbed my facial wash and then sat at our desk, investigating the ingredient list on the back of the bottle. Among the regular things like water and plant extract, it also included methylparaben and propylparaben. Aaron typed those two ingredients into Google and found a site called EWG.org (Environmental Working Group), which listed these as endocrine disruptors.

I stood over Aaron's shoulder as he continued to research about the endocrine system and its importance to the body. According to the American Medical Association's site, "Your endocrine system is a collection of glands that produce hormones that regulate your body's growth, metabolism, and sexual development and function. The hormones are released into the bloodstream and transported to tissues and organs throughout your body."[6]

"Aaron, do you really think that a face wash can keep my endocrine system from working?"

"I don't know, babe, but don't you think this sounds like it could be true? From what I'm reading, it looks like the endocrine system is valuable to the proper function of our bodies." He tapped the screen, which was now showing the FDA website. "This says that parabens have weak estrogen-like properties, but that the activity is much less than the body's naturally occurring estrogen." He read the screen some more. "This also says there isn't enough research to conclude that parabens are harmful, but the agency will continue to evaluate new data in this area.[7] It seems to me that there could be a connection, and who knows but maybe it affects people differently. Maybe you're just really sensitive to parabens."

Aaron's words made sense. If my body was somehow sensitive to parabens, and/or if the amount I was exposed to was a higher percentage than most, *could it be possible that the estrogen-mimicking parabens were disrupting my body's proper function?*

"Would you stop using this face wash so we can see if it changes anything?"

"No! I can't, Aaron, you don't understand. I had horrible acne, and this was the only thing that worked. I just can't! We don't even know if any of this is true."

"Jennifer, I would rather you have horrible acne and experience great sex than live the rest of our lives never knowing how good our sex life could be. You have to stop using this, just for a few weeks to see what happens."

I saw his reasoning, but I also knew the pain of acne! I argued with him, questioning his research and doubting that his discovery would lead us to better sex. I blindly assumed that if these parabens were affecting people, we would have heard about it on the news. But the more I struggled against it, the more I knew I should at least try. So reluctantly I agreed to give it up for a time.

Although my heart was stuffed full of fear about my skin potentially breaking out, I cared more about having a fulfilled marriage. We were a month and a half from our four-year anniversary and had experienced only a handful of semi-successful sexual encounters. After all that time of searching for a reason and a cure, I was skeptical about trying such an out-of-the-box theory. I took my bottle of face wash and set it on the counter, praying protection over my skin and hoping this would be the miracle cure we had searched for.

❁   ❁   ❁

About three days after I stopped using the face wash, I noticed a change in my body. Although I was still skeptical about being healed just because I stopped using a certain product, I couldn't deny the feeling I was experiencing. It was enough to call my husband, who was already at work.

"Babe, I don't want you to get too excited, but I feel different *down there*."

"Really?" His tone immediately became enthusiastic. "Do you think it was the face wash? Do you really feel that much of a difference?"

"Well, remember when I told you I was feeling numb down there and how I never really felt aroused?"

"Yeah." I could hear the excitement in his voice growing.

"Maybe the parabens were blocking me from feeling what I'm supposed to . . . I don't really know, I shouldn't have said anything. It was a big enough change to make me want to share it with you, but I'll keep watching to see how things change."

"That's great, babe! I really hope this is it!"

"Me too. Okay, I'll let you get back to work. I love you."

"I love you too!"

It was a short and awkward conversation for me, because I wasn't completely sure why my body was acting so differently, and I wasn't convinced it was because I'd stopped using my face wash. Although I had been practicing being unveiled with my husband, I still felt shy when it came to discussing my body with him.

This was the first moment I recognized a physical change with my body. I wanted to believe God had heard my cries, granting me an answer to my prayers. That night, Aaron was obviously ready to test out his theory. As much as I desperately desired to experience great sex, I asked him to wait a little longer. I didn't want my excitement over this change to be depleted if we tried and were unsuccessful. We did enjoy each other and expressed our love outwardly, only we intentionally avoided intercourse. And over and over I pleaded with God, *Please let this be it!*

⊛　⊛　⊛

Over the next three days, I monitored my body for any changes and we continued to avoid placing pressure on ourselves for initiating intercourse. Some of the bodily changes, such as wetness caused by natural lubrication, were very noticeable because I hadn't experienced them in years. My womanly parts felt revived!

As I explained these changes to my husband, he could not have been more thrilled. It was the extreme opposite to what he was feeling just a week prior. He lit up with hope and confidence.

That night as the sun went down, Aaron and I headed to our bedroom. We felt intimately connected as we talked about how the changes in my body were a sign of true healing. We even talked about what it might feel like to actually be able to consummate our marriage, which motivated both of us to want to try. Taking our time facing the obstacle that was before us, we held each other as Aaron prayed, "God, please let my wife and me be one. Please let us have great sex with no pain. We thank You for this miracle. Amen."

I whispered back, "Amen."

Aaron kissed me as if it were the first time we had ever kissed. I felt wanted and loved unconditionally. I was so thankful that God gifted me with such a patient man to endure this life with. I focused my attention on silently encouraging my muscles to relax.

And this time as we continued past where we would have stopped before, everything worked. No pain, no discomfort.

I started to cry from the overflow of joy bursting from my heart.

When Aaron noticed the tears, he panicked. "Are you okay?"

"No, no, I'm fine! I'm just so happy, babe. I can't believe this is what sex is like!"

Aaron took a deep sigh of relief and marveled aloud at all we had been missing. That moment was so precious. It was everything I had hoped for during our honeymoon!

The ecstasy we experienced as we physically became one flesh was more than satisfying. I am so thankful for the revelation God gave Aaron about my face wash and the toxic ingredients inside of it. And I'm so grateful for the restoration I experienced in my body. This breakthrough was exactly what I needed to know that sex was worth trying for and worth fighting for! I began to look forward to sex and enjoyed finding creative ways to maximize our pleasure. I praised God that our sex life, something I dreaded, was now redeemed. Aaron and I made up for the years we missed out on sexual intimacy, and I felt as if we were newlyweds for the first time . . . again. This breakthrough also renewed my faith in God, proving to me how much He cares about us. I suppose God gave us the answer earlier, using Joanne to bring us to the discovery of that answer. If only we had listened back then!

With that discovery, I chose not to stop at just the face wash, but became eager to get rid of every product with parabens listed as an ingredient. I quickly switched many of my personal care products to ones with more natural ingredients, including lotion, shampoo, conditioner, mascara, lubrication, and body wash. Aaron and I became advocates for paraben-free products, sharing with our family and friends the discovery we had stumbled upon. I specifically told Joanne how her friend's story was the inspiration for our discovery, and we praised God together for the way He fit all the pieces perfectly to help us on our journey. (For a full list of product reviews and what I use now, check out unveiledwife. com/healthy-products.) I found an assortment of new products that were healthy to use on my body, and surprisingly, I never had another acne breakout.

It was during this time that God unveiled to me how aggressive the enemy is in attacking marriages. For years Aaron and I fought and anguished over our relationship, finally figuring out that our number one issue was a result of our tainted environment.

We can't be the only couple who has struggled with this, I thought. *How many other wives struggle with this issue or something similar because of harmful chemicals?* Perhaps because my longest and deepest yearning had been fulfilled or maybe because the crazy connection we made sparked something in my heart, I noticed that my perspective was shifting. I started to feel a burden for the marriages of others who were in painful situations like ours, marriages on the edge of collapse. My heart hurt for them, wanting to comfort them without even knowing them. I began to pray for husbands and wives who were facing divorce, and I asked God to unveil truth to them just as He had for us.

❁ ❁ ❁

Although my husband and I experienced a breakthrough in our sex life after avoiding parabens, restoration and healing took months, and in many respects I am still recovering. As much as I appreciated being able to experience the most intimate act a husband and wife can share together, I had four years of pain and anxiety that needed to be undone.

When Aaron and I approached sex, I faced a mental battle of anticipating that our encounter would cause discomfort. Aaron could tell when I was tensing up and would approach sex with the utmost respect and gentleness. Despite his warm invitations, my anxiety often kept me from initiating sex with my husband, as well as arousing inhibitions that far outweighed my desire for sex. Even as I write this, I still struggle with anxieties about sex, thinking that it might cause me pain. Yet with each sexual experience my husband and I find painless and enjoyable, God reassures and reminds me of the healing He has brought. As my confidence grows, my anxieties shrink, making each act of intimacy easier than the last.

>> ———— *Behind the Veil* ————>

1. My husband offered an opinion that had the potential of radically impacting our ability to have sex, and my first response was rejection and resistance. I was motivated that way because of fear and uncertainty. Has your husband ever offered an opinion that you rejected or resisted because of fear? In what ways could his opinion positively or negatively affect your marriage?

2. Through Joanne's suggestion that we check out our environment to see if anything there might be causing the problem, God revealed the significant answer to our prayers. Yet for months we chose not to consider that option. We were not good listeners! What have you been praying earnestly for? Are you spending time "listening" for His answer? Is it possible God is using someone to provide that answer but you haven't been willing to consider that option? Why or why not?

3. After we received physical healing, the mental battle of thinking sex would hurt still influenced our sex life. In what ways does your mind influence the quality of your sex life?

CHAPTER 28
Unveiled

After our dramatic and dark escalation of struggles, God defended our marriage by protecting us from divorce, walking my husband and me through intense healing as He began to rewire my mind, body, and heart. But not only in the sexual area. God used our greatest marital struggle to confront me daily to change attitudes, habits, expectations, and other weaknesses, pressing upon my heart a passion for my character to reflect His holy character. Although I naively thought our marriage would miraculously be perfect after we were able to have sex, that wasn't the case! Our relationship did improve, but God had to help us battle and overcome our misperceptions and selfishness. God was refining us, using our marriage to drag our darkness into His light, knowing that the exposure to the truth would transform us.

My growing pains were excruciating. However, God revealed a powerful message to me that I clung to and reflected upon because it fed my soul indescribable hope. During a quiet time spent with God, I came across 2 Corinthians 3:16-18:

> Whenever anyone turns to the Lord, the veil is taken away. Now the Lord is the Spirit, and where the Spirit of the Lord is, there is freedom. And we all, who with

unveiled faces contemplate the Lord's glory, are being transformed into his image with ever-increasing glory, which comes from the Lord, who is the Spirit. (NIV)

God spoke to me through His Word, pointing out that this was the journey I was on with Him. As I offered to make myself known to God and known to my husband, I was being unveiled. Through that process of revealing His truth to me, God was transforming me, and this verse explained how and why He was doing it! That word *unveiled* resonated with me, as if it defined part of my purpose in being a Christian and a wife.

Interestingly, in the moment I read that verse, I remembered writing this specific word down many years before when I was in high school. A spike of adrenaline and excitement for the way God stirs pulled me out of my chair, and I ran to a notebook I had kept that was filled with old poems and other writing samples I was saving. I never could part with the words I wrote down, even if they were written on a napkin in crayon! I flipped through the binder page by page until my eyes landed on that sweet word: *unveiled*. Handwritten on a small piece of paper, tucked away for years, this message had incubated in my heart and I never knew. I continued to ponder the meaning of this word, asking God to reveal more to me, and He was faithful. (Read an additional meaning of the word *unveiled* in appendix A.)

God began to show me how He pursued me relentlessly. He desired a deeply intimate relationship with me, and even when I pushed Him away, He never gave up showing me His great love and lavishing it upon me.

When I accepted Jesus Christ as Lord and Savior, believing in the power of His death and resurrection, a veil was lifted from my heart and I experienced freedom, just as that verse mentioned. I was also given access to an intimate relationship with the Lord, thus marking the beginning of transformation. Although I was saved by grace, over time I had woven together another veil, made of expectations, imperfections, and insecurities! It served as a "security blanket" as I tried to hide my heart from the world, desperately avoiding any possible way of experiencing hurt. God pursued me amid my darkness, I responded to Him by turning my heart back toward Him, and He took this veil away piece by piece. God unveiled me and I was transformed by His Holy Spirit. Transformation continues in me as a result of abiding in Christ every day.

God took this concept one step further and revealed to me a beautiful similarity. I thought of a traditional bride who wears a long veil that covers her face. The veil remains in place until she stands before her husband at the altar and becomes his wife. When that bride is unveiled on her wedding day, it is expected that she remains unveiled throughout her marriage.

Through that image, God was showing me the importance of authenticity and vulnerability, a place where true intimacy resides. My desire to experience extraordinary intimacy with God and with my husband would be attainable, but it required me to remain unveiled.

My flesh and my spirit still battle; they always will. However, with the veil lifted I could see God more clearly, I could see my character more clearly, and I could see my husband more clearly. Without my vision being impaired, I realized how much I truly need God to remain at the center of my life. Although I was terrified of letting God, my husband, or others know the real me, I asked Him to help me live by faith and not by fear. And again, He was faithful. This concept of being unveiled was awe-inspiring. I thought about it day in and day out as God used it to walk me through specific heart issues I was wrestling with, and slowly He set me free.

>> ———— *Behind the Veil* ————→

1. One of the most important things I've learned is that I cannot be unveiled and I cannot know true love if I do

not know God. But when I've come to God openly and willingly, He has given me the courage to unveil myself to Him and to my husband. Do you need to get to know God? Are there aspects of your character in need of rewiring? If so, what's keeping you from giving them to God and asking Him to give you a healthy perception of marriage woven together by the threads of His love story? Will you ask Him to help your marriage reflect the good news of grace, the powerful gospel through which people encounter salvation, restoration, and reconciliation?

2. My veil, the "security blanket" I thought was keeping me from being hurt, was actually doing more damage by acting as a barrier, keeping me from experiencing real intimacy. It rested over my eyes, distorting my perspective of myself, of God, and of marriage. Do you have a veil distorting your views? Are you hiding behind a "security blanket," hoping not to get hurt? Why is living veiled more dangerous than living unveiled?

3. When you submit to God and turn toward Him, He will lift the veil and transform you into His likeness. Every part of your testimony, your journey with God, and your marriage, is significantly valuable—the good moments, the difficult ones, all of it. Nothing you have done in your past or in your marriage is too great a sin to be redeemed, nor can it stain God's reputation. The beauty of God's love story is His unfailing, unconditional, gracious, merciful, and eternal love for you and your husband, for me and my husband, for everyone. Have you submitted completely to God, asking Him to redeem your past failures, your journey, and your marriage? What's keeping you from submitting completely?

CHAPTER 29
Confronting the Heart Issues

As a new wife, I struggled with three major heart issues, which became the root causes for many of the problems Aaron and I faced. Those three threads, woven together, created the "security blanket" I mentioned—expectations, imperfections, and insecurities. These three areas kept my heart covered, hindering intimacy from thriving. God had a lot of work to do to transform me to be the person He desired. Part of the transformation process God walked me through involved acknowledging these heart issues and how my subsequent behavior contributed to the contention I encountered in my marriage.

❊　❊　❊

I had a plethora of marriage expectations that were formed as far back as early childhood. Many of those expectations were veiled, hidden in the deep places of my heart. For years I justified my notions of life and marriage, unaware of the devastating effects of those expectations if left unmet.

Entering marriage with such high expectations set my husband and me up for ruin. For example, trusting in my husband to be *my everything* was one of the most detrimental ways I hurt our marriage. I set my husband up for failure when I expected him to fulfill me completely. When I wanted to feel worthy, I sought my worthiness in my husband. When I wanted to feel loved unconditionally, I sought love from my husband. When I wanted to feel comforted, cherished, validated, or encouraged, I sought those things in my husband and *only* in my husband. However, because my husband is human and prone to sin, inevitably he let me down and could not fulfill my needs completely. And in those times, I felt unworthy and unloved.

While some expectations are good—for example, I expect my husband to be faithful to me—when they move into unrealistic and unattainable places, they become destructive. My expectations were so lofty they hurt him. Aaron could never be my everything—he was never designed to be! And whenever I tried to make him fit that role, I unintentionally placed him as an idol above God, believing that he had the capacity to do more for me than God Himself.

With the strain Aaron and I were experiencing, we tended to be overly sensitive to conflict. It did not take much for us to offend each other, and I am embarrassed to admit I took advantage of retaliating when I felt I deserved something I was not receiving. When I became aware of any opportunity to point out fault, I didn't hesitate to blame him. I complained about our living situation, about not having enough, about having only one car, about our finances, about our sexless life, about my husband's flaws, about work, about *anything* I deemed worthy of complaint. Those unmet expectations flowed over into discontentment, which too often I nursed in my heart.

Not only did discontentment grow, but pride did as well, which grew into a sense of entitlement: *I deserve better than this.* And that mentality seeped not only into my marriage, but into my relationship with God. Unmet expectations of God's role in my life lit a fire of anger within me. I believed being a daughter of the King meant that I would receive the best of everything. When it seemed as if God didn't intervene, that anger spread like a wildfire, consuming everything inside me, including my faith. I had high expectations for God to do the things I wanted, unable to grasp that God was more concerned about my character than my comfort. But in the midst of my pain and self-centered complaining, I exhausted my husband and I believe I saddened God.

After I spent several years repeating this same offense and suffering the consequences, God opened my eyes to the destruction of unmet expectations. God needed to transform me. He could do that only as I humbled myself and let go of my unrealistic and unmet expectations. Each time God humbled me, He used that experience to mold my attitude and character to reflect that of Christ and to shape my expectations to more closely align with His, which in all honesty are better than what I could ever dream of.

The transformation I underwent didn't happen immediately. Rather, the process was spread out over time as I sought to know God and make myself known to Him—a process that continues to mature me every day.

Joy and contentment defend me from the barrage of unmet expectations. If I don't have joy, those notions wreak havoc in my heart, turning it against the ones I love. I know because it happened countless times. It took me years of suffering and loathing in self-pity, guilt, and brokenness even to begin to understand the power of pure joy.

Joy springs up where contentment thrives, and contentment is produced through sincere thankfulness. The greatest constant I have found to help sustain me and give me strength and hope no matter what the circumstance is to cling to the joy of the Lord. God's Word tells me, "Don't be dejected and sad, for the joy of the Lord is your strength!" (Nehemiah 8:10).

God taught me how to be thankful by sharing specific things I am grateful for with God and with my husband. As thankfulness fills my heart to the brim with contentment, I find myself living with extraordinary joy, regardless of unmet expectations or circumstances or past hurts.

❀   ❀   ❀

The second heart issue I had to face was my imperfections. God used my marriage to unveil my sin and my imperfections, giving me the opportunity to repent and change. Before I was a wife, I never would have been aware of certain sin in my life. I had a skewed perception of who I was, hiding my struggles behind a veil to appear good—a lie I tricked myself into believing because I desired to be perfect. I had defined who I was based only on pieces of how I was performing. I feared that if people—including my husband— knew the whole me, imperfections and all, they wouldn't like me, I wouldn't like me, and worst of all, I would misrepresent God. I thought if I claimed to be a Christian, I had the responsibility to be a good person because I was representing God and His gospel. I didn't want to stain His story. And in my mind, for too many years I believed that struggling in my marriage was a stain. Unfortunately, as I aimed to be good and pretended to be when I wasn't, I missed one of the most significant pieces of God's story: His amazing grace.

I had to stop living in denial and face the reality of who I really was in order to become who God desired me to be. It took me years to comprehend that I was messed up, imperfect, full of sin, yet redeemed by God's gift of grace—that being transparent with who I *really* am doesn't stain God's gospel; it reflects His sovereignty more clearly. My testimony is that I am a sinner, forgiven and transformed by the atoning sacrifice of Jesus Christ, and the power in sharing that story is to let others know that they can have that testimony too.

As God opened my eyes and allowed me the freedom to be transparent with myself, my imperfections were unveiled, and I felt the power of God's grace. Although experiencing God's extraordinary compassion has been remarkable, seeing my true reflection has been torturous. Author Gary Thomas recognizes that feeling. In *Sacred Marriage*, Gary shares this quote from a couple named Gary and Betsy Ricucci to illustrate how marriage works to uncover and force us to face our imperfections: "One of the best wedding gifts God gave you was a full-length mirror called your spouse. Had there been a card attached, it would have said, 'Here's to helping you discover what you're *really* like!'"[8]

My husband has been my full-length mirror. The moment I look to blame him, I see my sin staring back at me. Big, ugly, messed up, crazy blemishes that are difficult to ignore or cover up. God has strategically used my husband to reveal my sin to me. Little by little I've identified areas that have needed adjusting, but it was not always a smooth transition. Time and time again, seeing my sin infuriated me. I didn't want to see it, and I wasn't ready or prepared to confront any of it. Contrary to my vows of enduring love and kindness, I said yes in my marriage to impurity, deception, selfishness, manipulation, accusation, idolatry, withholding, apathy, and more.

So much of the sin I struggled with was intertwined with other sin. It has been difficult to retrain my behavior with regard to individual sins when one response toward my husband involves several of them simultaneously. For example, if my husband fails to meet an expectation and I allow it to offend me because I am not seeking my fulfillment in God (idolatry), my response comes from a selfish perspective, motivated by a manipulating posture to get him to do what I want, perpetuated by a lie that I am right and he is wrong (pride), all of which comes bursting out of my mouth with malicious words purposed to make him hurt in the same way I am convinced I hurt.

As much as I don't like it, my husband responds with those precious properties of a mirror. When I sin, it negatively affects my husband, and his response is an integral part of helping me realize I made a mistake. Although those moments are difficult to endure for both of us, they contribute to shaping our characters.

❀　❀　❀

I may be subject to the impediment of my flesh, but there is another part of who I am, my spirit. The inner conflict between my flesh and spirit is an ongoing battle. Every choice I make, every action, every word dictates whether I am operating in the flesh or the spirit. My flesh is susceptible to sin, constantly seeking to fulfill desires regardless of consequences, deficient in appropriate strategies, often impairing relationships around me. For example, when I fail to keep my sin nature in check, insecurities grow wildly, convincing me of my faults and my brokenness, that getting married was a mistake and that depression is my only option, all while my husband suffers the abuse of manipulation, jealousy, and rejection. These are all flaming arrows aimed at destroying intimacy.

Every sin starts within a person's heart, conceived by thoughts of selfishness. Sin is birthed by intention and matures through actions. Accepting the truth that I can still so easily sin has been difficult for me. I knew I had room to improve when communicating with my husband, but I never would have believed that I was capable of offending my husband through idolatry and impure thoughts of another. But I am and I did sin in that way. Although my sin never matured into a physical affair, I understand more clearly how a husband or wife can follow through with such sin. It all begins by entertaining thoughts of selfishness. Regardless of the sins I saw as minimal or shocking, *all* sin is severe because it severs intimacy.

Sin and selfishness are not conducive to a good marriage. God's design of a holy covenant between a man and a woman requires us to live out the "each other" Scriptures, guidelines for cultivating a healthy, intimate relationship in any context.

I am giving you a new commandment: Love each other.
Just as I have loved you, you should love each other.
JOHN 13:34

Love each other with genuine affection, and take delight in honoring each other.
ROMANS 12:10

Live in harmony with each other. Don't be too proud to enjoy the company of ordinary people. And don't think you know it all!

ROMANS 12:16

Always be humble and gentle. Be patient with each other, making allowance for each other's faults because of your love.

EPHESIANS 4:2

Be kind to each other, tenderhearted, forgiving one another, just as God through Christ has forgiven you.

EPHESIANS 4:32

Submit to one another out of reverence for Christ.

EPHESIANS 5:21

You must warn each other every day, while it is still "today," so that none of you will be deceived by sin and hardened against God.

HEBREWS 3:13

These verses are instructions that will help create a loving atmosphere in marriage—which will not occur if my husband and I are motivated by sin and selfishness, and it certainly won't occur if I deny my imperfections and dwell on my supposed entitlements.

My sin was ripping apart the foundation Aaron and I had committed to on our wedding day. Sin that is unrepentant is as untamed as a hurricane thrashing against the land. If we hadn't been intentional about eradicating sin, it would have completely destroyed our marriage.

I was missing the point that marriage is about oneness. We were separated in our intimacy, separated in our finances, separated in our relationships with God, and we were being separated more and more by our sin, by *my* sin.

The revelations and reflections of sin did not come in days or even weeks, but rather over years of living with my full-length mirror. However, amid the pain of severed intimacy caused by sin, God gave my husband and me to each other to redeem our character and our love. I learned that lesson in an unusual way.

❀ ❀ ❀

One year Aaron traveled to South America for two weeks. During that separation I pressed into God and begged Him to draw close to me. God directed me to study John 13, in which Jesus washed His disciples' feet, such an intimate expression of honor. After Jesus finished, He told His disciples, "Since I, your Lord and Teacher, have washed your feet, you ought to wash each other's feet. I have given you an example to follow. Do as I have done to you" (John 13:14-15).

When my husband arrived home at 5:30 a.m., I jumped out of bed to greet him. I had a renewed perspective, and I was eager to do as Jesus did. I explained to my husband all that the Lord had taught me, and I apologized for my negative behavior prior to his departure. I read John 13 to Aaron and concluded by sharing that I felt God asking me to lay down my sin and seek to be a wife who has a Christlike character. Then I invited my husband into the bathroom where I washed his feet. In that instance, I affirmed my husband. And the unexpected reward I received was over-whelming. Although the experience was awkward, I was amazed to witness the immediate impact it had on our marriage. We both began to talk more freely and intimately. The humility required to submit and serve is a quality that is returned with respect and appreciation. It had the power to soften both of our hearts— a power that far outweighed what I believed about control.

Sin hinders intimacy, but forgiveness restores it. Sin hinders intimacy, but love redeems it. Sin, imperfections, and blemishes in my character are inevitable. Not one of us is perfect, except Jesus Christ. The acknowledgment of this truth was challenging to accept—especially in my role as a wife. It was imperative that I allow God to use my husband to unveil my sin to me. As I was confronted, instead of pointing the finger with blame or manipulation, I was able to rebuke the sin, take responsibility for my fault, repent, and witness the phenomenon of transformation through the power of amazing grace. If I had not experienced a heart of repentance, my sin would have continued to grow and take over my life, leading me down a path of more pain and complete separation from God and from my husband.

Fostering a character of humility emulates Christ and His perfect love—the kind of love that binds a husband and wife to God in peace, strength, and unity. This happens in that moment of surrender, that juncture of apology and forgiveness. If my husband sins against me, my part is to extend forgiveness. If I offend my husband or sin against him, it is my responsibility to reconcile through a humble apology. I'm so grateful that I can do this not from my own strength, but through Christ's:

> Anyone who belongs to Christ has become a new person. The old life is gone; a new life has begun! And all of this is a gift from God, who brought us back to himself through Christ. And God has given us this task of reconciling people to him. For God was in Christ, reconciling the world to himself, no longer counting people's sins against them. And he gave us this wonderful message of reconciliation.
>
> 2 CORINTHIANS 5:17-19

❀ ❀ ❀

The third heart issue God revealed to me was my insecurity. The seam that bound my husband and me on our wedding day was breaking apart over years of allowing my insecurity to lead my life. So many insecurities grew out of my past experiences and my expectations.

My parents' divorce, for instance, caused me to become insecure about unconditional love. And even after I got married and determined not to allow divorce to enter my relationship, those insecurities and fears continued to hang over me.

One of my biggest insecurities came out of our sexual struggles. I felt like a failure, broken and incompetent—perfect places for insecurity to breed and grow. And that insecurity led to a deep loneliness. I never would have thought I would feel lonely in marriage. In fact, I was convinced marriage would provide the exact opposite: a beautiful union between two lovers experiencing the rest of their lives together. In actuality, loneliness in marriage was worse than being single, because I had someone to spend a lifetime with, I had someone to share the warmth of my bed with, I had someone to be accountable to each and every day, but I didn't have a thriving marriage—and that brought about the worst kind of loneliness. And the cycle began again in which I felt lonely, which made me feel insecure, which caused me to withdraw, which led to more loneliness.

But it wasn't only loneliness in my marriage—I was lonely in my faith. I was shocked when I realized how miniscule my view of God was. Although I believed in Him, I struggled to accept how I could have an even deeper, more intimate relationship with Him. I rarely allowed myself to get close enough to Him as I let my expectations and insecurity determine our proximity.

Regrettably, there was a time when I almost turned my back completely, avoiding God as much as I possibly could, frustrated that He would not provide for me the perfect marriage or the perfect life. I was selfish, manipulative with God, stubbornly justifying my behavior through my hurt, just as I did when my dad didn't meet my expectations, just as I did when my husband didn't meet them. I gave more weight to insecurity and fear than I ever gave to the One I was hoping would save me from such despair. My faith was lacking, my marriage was failing, my life was miserable.

My husband often quotes his dad: "Some of the most miserable people are the ones who know God but choose not to follow Him." That was me. I chose insecurity, which led to misery with every decision I made, which in turn led to feeling isolated from God.

I am so thankful God never gave up on me! He pursued me passionately and gave me multiple opportunities to turn my heart back to Him. When I dismantled the barriers inside and embraced true intimacy—when I put my trust in God—I was able to push aside my insecurities to live according to the Spirit, who grants indescribable freedom.

Each time insecurity threatened to overtake me or my relationship, God walked with me and assured me the issues we were facing in marriage would refine me, if I allowed them to. This was not an easy process. *How could suffering and pain refine my character?* I often wondered. I may not have understood the trials I was enduring, but God was faithful in showing me how He could use a difficult situation to make me a better person.

The apostle James reminded me: "When troubles of any kind come your way, consider it an opportunity for great joy. For you know that when your faith is tested, your endurance has a chance to grow. So let it grow, for when your endurance is fully developed, you will be perfect and complete, needing nothing" (James 1:2-4).

The inner struggle between flesh and spirit is a constant reminder that there is something more, something greater than just the day at hand and the time I am given to spend. It is that contention that stirs my heart to question faith, but it is also that same contention that attacks my sacred well of hope.

Without hope and without faith I have no purpose. If I don't have purpose, I don't have any reason to strive to be better, to choose good, to be positive with the influence I have, or to care about the results that follow my actions. Without hope, how can I look forward to my husband being transformed into the man God created him to be, participating in His great love story by fulfilling his part in our relationship? Without faith, what motivation do I have to pray and ask God to empower my husband, free my husband, teach my husband, or transform my husband?

Insecurity robbed me of these opportunities and kept me so inwardly focused that I rarely took the time to intercede for my husband as I should have. Insecurity also kept my eyes focused on the negative about myself, leading me to believe the opposite of what God created me to be and convincing me that I would never be able to change. Insecurity told me that I was unworthy to be loved, causing my soul to seek validation and approval from my mom, my dad, my husband, and anyone else to whom I was close.

Insecurity is a stronghold the enemy has used to tempt me to sin and lure me into depression to keep me ineffective for God's Kingdom, most importantly in my relationship with my husband. Insecurity is a stronghold my flesh has used to try to control my spirit. But not anymore! I choose to fight against insecurity and starve my fears! I choose to stand strong in faithfulness, the better defense mechanism to protect my heart and my marriage from the attacks that ravage marital relationships. It starts with faith. The Bible describes faith as "the confidence that what we hope for will actually happen; it gives us assurance about things we cannot see" (Hebrews 11:1).

God showed me the value of being a wife of faith, a wife who trusts Him wholeheartedly, who is confident of her worthiness and purpose. I choose to be a wife who believes she can change and believes her husband can be transformed into the man God designed him to be, and I choose to strive to affirm him in truthfulness.

I desire to be a wife of faith who can persevere no matter the circumstance because she is full of hope, which is the foundation of her motivation. I do not want fear to define what I do, nor let my flesh win the tug-of-war, nor let thick walls keep me isolated from experiencing true intimacy. I believe as I choose to walk in the Spirit, love will pour out and bless my marriage. With

God's help I can endure, I can have a thriving marriage, I can fight against my three heart influencers that threaten to keep me down—but it requires faith and hope.

>> ——————— *Behind the Veil* ———————→

1. One of the biggest reasons my husband and I experienced contention in those early years was because of unmet expectations. I constantly compared our reality to the ideal of perfection I desired. God showed me that a heart of thankfulness powerfully kills the bitterness and disappointment that try to spring up from unmet expectations. What are some unmet expectations you have about marriage? Now what are twice as many gifts of marriage you are thankful for? What is the contrast in feelings when you think about expectations versus thankfulness?

2. I thought I was close to perfect because I "did all the right things" growing up. After becoming a wife, I pointed the finger of blame at my husband often, convinced his sin was greater than mine. Sin had a grip on me and I didn't even know it! I am so appreciative that God used my marriage to show me my sin, and once I saw it, I wanted *even more* to be transformed. What kind of sin do you find in your life? In what ways has God used your marriage to show you your sin? What is reconciliation worth to you?

3. Fear is a crippling vice that motivates me to make decisions in which I neglect to trust God. Many times fear is what has kept me from experiencing a deeply intimate relationship with God and my husband. I learned that if I wanted my fears to dissipate, I needed to starve them by feeding my faith. What are some of your greatest fears about marriage?

What do you think God would say to encourage you to overcome these fears? What would your marriage look like if you operated out of faith and not fear?

4. I eventually learned that I alone did not have the power to fix my marriage. Trusting God and believing He had the power to heal me was a necessity. Do you believe God wants to heal you, or do you get caught up in trying to fix yourself or your marriage on your own? How does your behavior reflect what you believe?

CHAPTER 30

God's Masterpiece

As a child, I used to watch my mom work tirelessly on projects around the house. She would come home thrilled to have found treasures hiding in the trash, confident that she could rebuild, restore, or make something completely new out of the pieces she managed to collect. She always had a special way of seeing potential in the things that others deemed garbage. To this day her home is filled with workstations where she meticulously creates. Motivated by her vision of potential, she removes any hardware or unnecessary parts, strips and sands the surfaces, then fixes any damage she finds. From there she paints or stains and uses any other strategy to bring the waste she salvaged to new life. She is good at what she does; she's an artist by nature. I admire her talent to take something others discard and completely transform it into something beautiful.

At a time when I thought my marriage was disposable, God found me and saw my marriage as worthy. He knew the work involved to rebuild and restore the damage incurred over years of distress, but He didn't let that stop Him from pursuing my husband and me. His vision of our potential far outweighed anything I ever knew was possible. As the true artist He is, God took my marriage and transformed it into something magnificent.

Relationships are dynamic, especially a relationship with God and a relationship with a spouse. A marvelous complexity exists when two become one; and I do not think anyone has the capacity to understand or grasp that precious mystery in its entirety.

I may not have agreed in the midst of my struggles, but I can now attest that I believe God is good and His timing is best. I am learning to embrace this gift of marriage, the good moments as well as the difficult ones, trusting that God will use it all for His glory. During the four years Aaron and I lived in a sexless marriage, God taught us both a great deal about ourselves, things we can now appreciate after trudging through the mire—issues we were able to confront, which perhaps would still be lying unearthed in our hearts, secretly plotting against us.

I will have to continually confront all the things God has empowered me to overcome as they come back to test my character. The difference is now I can identify each one more quickly because I am no longer blinded by the veil that kept me from seeing these things, and because I implore God to help me overcome again, relying on Him more and more each day. Instead of faltering beneath the attacks of such warfare, I can stand firm in faith, because I have seen God's power and I am confident He will help me through it all. He was faithful before; I know I can trust Him to be faithful again and again.

As I abide in Jesus and remain in an intimate relationship with Him, He continues to provide revelations to me about Himself, about my life, and about marriage. I am grasping the truth that I am not defined by my past experiences, past choices, or past circumstances, and I am not defined by my sin. I am defined by Jesus, the testimony of His gospel, and what the Lord says about me in His Word. God is my everything, and I confidently confess that He is the only One who can ever truly fulfill and satisfy me.

Having this change of heart has shaped me to look at my relationship with my husband in a different light. No longer do I fully rely on a man who is prone to failing. And disappointment has lost its grip on me. With this incredible freedom and contentment, I see my husband as God sees Him—and when I see my husband as God sees him, my attitude toward him mirrors God's as well. The entire atmosphere of our relationship becomes set according to a standard the Designer always intended.

As God unveiled me before Himself and before my husband, I encountered a transcending peace and strength. I believe God was equipping me and increasing my faith to help me persevere. He was reminding me of His great love for me, He was reaffirming my value, He was healing me from the inside out, and He was encouraging me that my marriage was worth fighting for. God pursued me relentlessly, and in my response of turning toward Him, He held me in a firm embrace, magnificently molding my character, like clay in a potter's hands. To this day, He continues to shape me as His masterpiece. As Paul says, "We are God's masterpiece. He has created us anew in Christ Jesus, so we can do the good things he planned for us long ago" (Ephesians 2:10).

Drawing closer to God has radically influenced my life. Over the years, I slowly began recognizing the positive changes in my husband and me, knowing without a doubt it was God's presence in our lives as we submitted to Him that was positively affecting our relationship. Each and every transformation added to the development of our characters to be more like Christ, which made us become all the more attracted to each other in the process. As much as we endured in those fresh years of marriage, I am thankful God used our situation for something extraordinary. Intimacy continues to flourish between God and me and between my husband and me as we seek to know each other and be made known.

And God has blessed us abundantly. The physical intimacy that was missing for our first four years was redeemed. It has become enjoyable for us—so much so that I got pregnant and gave birth to a handsome baby boy! Our marriage is ripening with age as we intentionally move closer to God and to each other.

Our marriage is fulfilled only because of Him! I suppose if everything had been perfect from the beginning, I would have had no need for God. I wouldn't have cried out to Him in desperation or surrendered to Him in an intimate way or been transformed or filled with the wisdom I now have. I would have missed out on getting to know God because I would still be clutching my veil. Blinded, I would have also missed out on seeing my husband for who he really is. However, I have changed so much because of the mess God allowed me to go through. The shift in my perspective and character has definitely been worth it all.

I feel strongly that the intimacy I have embraced with my husband would have occurred *regardless* of receiving physical healing, because of the deep connection I encountered through transparency and making myself fully known to him. That was the beautiful gift I received.

God prompted me to share our story. I was resistant at first, unsure if what I had to share was worthy. Despite my feelings, God pursued me, asking me to give an account of everything my husband and I had experienced in those first few years of marriage and the revelations He has revealed to me along the way. My prayer is that all who read our story will hear echoes of the Kingdom of God. For throughout each day that unfolded, God never left us. Although my heart turned hard at times and my faith was lacking, God never abandoned us. My hope is that many other couples can find the courage to be patient among the pain, with faith that their marriage will be transformed and fulfilled, in God's timing.

❀　❀　❀

Marriage is a mosaic you build with your spouse—millions of tiny moments that create your love story. Every moment, whether difficult or enjoyable, is another splash of color contributing to the collaborative work of art that is your union of oneness. It can be easy to get caught up in circumstances or trials. However, if you can persevere just long enough, more and more pieces will be added to your portrait of marriage, laid by the hand of the Almighty. The key to admiring this mosaic is all about having a godly perspective!

Your marriage is important, your marriage has purpose, your marriage is worthy and worth fighting for. Your role as a wife is significant, and the responsibility bestowed with such an honorable position is immense. Please do not consider doing it by yourself or relying on your own wisdom and strength. Proverbs 3:5-6 encourages us, "Trust in the LORD with all your heart; do not depend on your own understanding. Seek his will in all you do, and he will show you which path to take."

I challenge you to surrender to God every day. Cultivate intimacy by seeking the mystery of your marriage to God, as well as your marriage to your husband. Remain unveiled.

Being an unveiled wife is about allowing God to reveal to you the contrast between your desires and His will. It is about refusing to let unmet expectations cripple your marriage, and it is about choosing joy over complaint. It is then that your perspective of God and marriage will be radically transformed. However, in the process of aligning your heart with God's, the contrast of your character to His becomes clearer. Being an unveiled wife requires recognition of your sin. It is about having a repentant heart determined never to do those things again, and it is about pursuing reconciliation in relationships. Being an unveiled wife is about confronting and crushing your fears; believing in truth more than in doubt, worry, or lies, and finding your security in God alone. When you have faith in God and you trust Him, then and only then will you be secure. You will experience God's peace, which actively protects and guards your precious heart.

An unveiled wife is real and transparent. She is authentic in what she does and what she says. An unveiled wife pursues love, joy, peace, patience, kindness, goodness, faithfulness, gentleness, and self-control (see Galatians 5:22-23). She surrenders her pride and lets down the walls of her heart, vulnerably trusting God with her life. In being unveiled she experiences God's grace and in turn extends grace in marriage. She allows God to transform her character with the purpose of reflecting His character.

God wants *you* to become an unveiled wife. Let God, your husband, and others get to know the real you!

Thank you for giving me the opportunity to make myself known. Being unveiled before you was not easy, but I believe God will use the words in this book to impress upon your heart His amazing love for you. He invites you to join Him on a journey of true intimacy that will radically impact you and your marriage. He stands at the altar, hoping you will say "I do."

Whether you are inspired to seek adventure, pray with your spouse, draw closer to God, get help for addiction, restore broken relationships, reconcile your past, find healing from environmental toxins, or remain faithful in your marriage, I pray that this moment is a milestone, preparing you for a season of extraordinary change! I urge you to vow today to be an unveiled wife and embrace intimacy with God and with your husband.

VOWS OF AN UNVEILED WIFE

I vow to submit to Christ, to receive Him as my Savior, to allow Him to wash me with His Word and wash my stains away.

I vow to lay down my expectations of marriage and seek God's will above all else.

I vow to be sanctified, to allow God to reveal sin in my life and to repent of it.

I vow to live by faith, to let go of my insecurities and trust God.

I vow to love and respect my husband with my words and my actions.

I vow to pursue true intimacy with God and my husband.

I vow to be continually unveiled before God, my husband, and others so that Christ will be glorified.

I do.

Dear Lord,

Thank You for the woman reading this. I pray You would anoint her as she draws close to You. Reveal to her any unmet expectations she may be clinging to in her relationship with You or with her husband. Align her heart to Yours and free her from the strain of frustration or resentment. I pray this wife is able to face her sins unafraid. Fill her with courage and a passion to be the woman You created her to be. I pray she is able to confront these imperfections and turn her heart toward You. I pray You would redeem her and transform her. I pray she is able to receive Your gift of grace, as well as to forgive herself. Take away her anxiety and help her to see that You are the only One who can fulfill her completely. I pray against the attacks of the enemy as well as the attacks from her flesh. Go before her, walk beside her, and at times may You carry her to help her persevere. Remind her every day of her value and worthiness. I pray this wife understands her purpose in Your amazing will. Be her Defender, her Refuge, her Everything! In Jesus' name, amen!

Behind the Veil

1. God knew I desired to have sex with my husband. What I didn't realize, but now understand, is that God wanted more than just a great sex life for me; God wanted to transform me. Just as a person can't just use a bandage to cover up a major cut without cleaning it first, God knew more than I did about my heart and the deep-seated issues that needed to be cleaned before I could be healed. When I humbled myself before God, He unveiled me and transformed these

areas. My flesh and my spirit still battle—they always will. However, with the veil lifted I can see more clearly how much I truly need God at the center of my life. Is God the center of your life? Are you willing to open your heart to Him so that He can transform you?

2. Being unveiled has allowed me to embrace true intimacy with God and with my husband, satisfying my deep needs for love and acceptance. In what ways is this message of being unveiled moving your heart to embrace true intimacy in your relationships?

3. God turned my mourning into rejoicing and showed me how sharing my story can help others in their marriage journey. Are you willing to share your story with others around you? What parts of your story reflect the awesome glory of God that could inspire someone to have hope in what God is doing?

A True Love Story

The groom walked down the aisle with joy set before Him,
each step taken in utter confidence of the holy matrimony that would unify Him and His bride. The pressures
of the world rested on His shoulders, baggage He would put to
death with the covenant of marriage.

This was no ordinary wedding. In fact, it caught many people
by surprise. Although there were no cordial invitations welcoming
guests, witnesses lined the aisle experiencing the power of true love.

The groom desired so much for His bride, including a new
life where shame could no longer grip her heart, where her security could not be shaken by any earthly forces, and where a truly
intimate grace-filled relationship prevailed. He knew His part in
the love story: He would finish His walk and hang up His life as a
single man. His passion proved His enduring love. Stretching His
arms out wide, He showed every guest present and every generation to come just how much He adored His bride. He cherished
her in a mighty way no other man ever could or ever would. A
legacy of perfect love.

Motivated by truth, Christ was nailed to a cross. Despite His
anguish and the pain radiating throughout His entire body, His
thoughts were for His bride. He saw His bride in all her glory,

knowing in faith that she would be united with Him for eternity. The bride of Jesus Christ is the church, those who believe in Him and receive Him as Lord and Savior. In an instant of surrender, a willingness to lay down one's life for another, came the redemption of man, reconciliation between God and His creation, a precious and holy new covenant.

The story of Jesus Christ is one of power. His purpose was clear, prophesied and recorded before He was even born. God humbled Himself and became bound by a human body for the sake of humankind. He desired to reconcile with His creation, but in order to do so, a sacrifice would need to be made. However, not just any sacrifice would be sufficient to be an atoning sacrifice to pay for the sins of all. The cost was too great. The only one capable of paying such a debt was God Himself.

⊛ ⊛ ⊛

Jesus walked this earth as 100 percent man and 100 percent God. He experienced the battle between flesh and spirit. Yet regardless of how He was tempted, He never sinned. Jesus Christ lived a perfect life, a life that was pleasing to God.

Jesus was motivated to fulfill His purpose because of His love for people, even those who He knew would betray Him or turn their backs on Him. Compassion comprised His character, woven through every fiber of His being. He healed the sick, the lame, and the blind. He fed the hungry. He invested truth by sharing the message of God with those around Him. He served others in humility and was intentional about building intimate relationships with people because He cared for them deeply. His story is powerful because it reveals love, grace, and faith. The way He led His life has been an example for others to live by for thousands of years. He was a great man, completely flawless, absolutely miraculous.

Although Jesus was a perfect man, His purpose was yet to be fulfilled. The time came when He was betrayed, arrested, and convicted. His penalty was death. Jesus was stripped, spit upon, beaten, and cursed. His flesh was pierced and injuries mounted as He was mocked over and over. He bore the weight of the world's sin, yet His posture reflected the confidence He had in God's will. The groom hung up His life for the sake of His bride.

The unconditional love poured out that day was and still stands unprecedented. The marriage of Christ and His bride, the church, is a beautiful story, a perfect example for husbands and wives to model in their own marital relationships. Ephesians 5:21-33 is where the powerful correlation between the earthly covenant of marriage and the new covenant of marriage through Christ really shines:

Submit to one another out of reverence for Christ.

Wives, submit yourselves to your own husbands as you do to the Lord. For the husband is the head of the wife as Christ is the head of the church, his body, of which he is the Savior. Now as the church submits to Christ, so also wives should submit to their husbands in everything.

Husbands, love your wives, just as Christ loved the church and gave himself up for her to make her holy, cleansing her by the washing with water through the word, and to present her to himself as a radiant church, without stain or wrinkle or any other blemish, but holy and blameless. In this same way, husbands ought to love their wives as their own bodies. He who loves his wife loves himself. After all, no one ever hated their own body, but they feed and care for their body, just as Christ does the church—for we are members of his body. "For this reason a man will leave his father and mother and be united to his wife, and the two will become one flesh." This is a profound mystery—but I am talking about Christ and the church. However, each one of you also must love his wife as he loves himself, and the wife must respect her husband. (NIV)

206 || THE UNVEILED WIFE

Jesus left His Father in heaven and His mother on earth to be united to His wife, the church. And through the power of the Holy Spirit's indwelling, the two become one. Jesus and I are one as He lives in me. This profound mystery leaves me in awe and adoration. These Scriptures also challenge me in my role as a wife, inspiring me to model my marriage just as Jesus exemplified.

One part of this Scripture has always been intriguing, yet hard to receive: the part that describes how Christ gave Himself up for His bride to make her holy, to present her as radiant and blameless, without stain, wrinkle, or blemish. This is the longing deep within the hearts of women, evident in our relentless search to be beautiful, wrinkle-free, and utterly perfect. I wish I had let God's words sink deep into my soul and saturate my whole self from an early age. Instead I stood at arm's length, in disbelief that love had the power to do all that. I was convinced my faults were too big to be washed away.

Growing up, I feared letting people know who I really was, sin and all, because I considered myself a representative of the gospel, an ambassador, and I did not want my true self to stain the perfection of Christ. So I hid beneath a covering I desperately hoped would reflect God's pure image. Unfortunately, I was missing a pivotal part of God's message: the power of His amazing grace, the very gift that attracts hearts to Him, the very gift that heals our brokenness.

I should have allowed Jesus to fulfill His role in my life and wash me with His Word; I should have believed He had the authority to wash away my stains. I sang those worship songs at church, I felt the lyrics I sang about Jesus washing me white as snow, but I clung to my veil as a security blanket, afraid of what being unveiled as a bride of Christ would truly mean.

❀   ❀   ❀

The sky grew dark and His heart was weary. At the very moment Christ took His last breath, a veil was torn: "And behold, the veil of the temple was torn in two from top to bottom; and the earth shook and the rocks were split" (Matthew 27:51, NASB).

This veil was a sacred garment that hung in the holy Tabernacle and later in the Temple. Before Christ died on that cross, the veil served as a barrier to protect the Holy of Holies, God's dwelling place, from the plight of a dark world. The veil stood nearly sixty feet tall, thirty feet wide, and four inches thick.[9] The veil shielded people from God, separating His perfect presence from the people's sin. Only once a year on a specific day was the high priest allowed to enter past the veil to offer an animal sacrifice for the atonement of sin.

God's will for Jesus was to be the final sacrifice once and for all, an act of redemption that would reconcile man and woman to their Creator. At the moment of Jesus' death, the veil in the Temple was torn from the top to the bottom, a feat that only God Himself could have done. It was as if He gripped it in His strong hands and ripped the raiment in His anguish. God grieved the death and separation of His only begotten Son.

The threads of a garment that were so heavily and intricately pieced together lay frayed and fallen, a representation of Jesus Christ, whose body was broken, removing the barriers from believers and giving humans access to God through the precious blood of Jesus. God let His walls down for us, an act of true love, selfless love, fearless love. Believing in Jesus Christ is the only way to experience intimacy with God.

❊   ❊   ❊

This veil is also significant because it represents exposure to the truth. When a person believes Christ's love story, His death and resurrection, the veil is lifted from his or her heart. Whenever anyone turns to the Lord, the veil is taken away. The apostle Paul describes it this way:

> Since we have such a hope, we are very bold. We are not
> like Moses, who would put a veil over his face to prevent

the Israelites from seeing the end of what was passing away. But their minds were made dull, for to this day the same veil remains when the old covenant is read. It has not been removed, because only in Christ is it taken away. Even to this day when Moses is read, a veil covers their hearts. But whenever anyone turns to the Lord, the veil is taken away.

2 CORINTHIANS 3:12-16, NIV

I have been a Christian since I was a young child. In middle school I gained a greater understanding of God and experienced intimacy in my relationship with Him. I was unveiled as a bride of Christ. However, as I grew up and especially after I entered marriage, I unknowingly had been weaving together another veil. I wove together various threads of expectations, imperfections, and insecurities to cover myself and keep others from knowing who I was because I was so afraid of misrepresenting God and also to protect myself from hurt.

The veil I pieced together guarded my heart from my husband and kept me separated from intimacy with God. I was not bold in my faith, rather I was suffering silently behind a sheer facade. But in the depths of my despair, when my marriage was failing and my heart was frail, I turned to the Lord and He removed the veil. I experienced indescribable freedom and peace. I finally began to understand that my faults and weaknesses would never stain the gospel, but rather they would show the gospel's power! This was God's grace!

My fear kept me from experiencing the richness of God's grace for years. In light of my journey with God, I looked at the church as a wife herself and what I found astounded me. The bride of Christ seems to be on a similar path I was on: controlled by a root of fear dealing with issues of expectations, imperfections, and insecurities. In my experience, the church has been so worried about staining the image of Christ's love story, it has at times removed the power of God's amazing grace. The church has hidden beneath a facade of "everything is perfect" while parts of her body suffer in silence.

My hope is that the bride of Christ can experience true freedom and peace as she allows Jesus to unveil her. In doing so she will learn to be transparent in her faults, weakness, and sin, and will expose the less-than-perfect parts of herself. Then she can be presented to Him as radiant, clothed in His grace—a garment whiter than any wedding dress. Utterly perfect, pleasing, and miraculous.

For the love story of Christ is a pure testimony of His great love for each of us. Since we each make up the bride, we have a great opportunity to experience what it means to be unveiled. While it is not always a comfortable process as we humble ourselves and become exposed, it is in that moment of allowing Him to lift the veil so that we see each other clearly that true intimacy thrives, grace overflows, compassion swells, freedom reigns, and incredible healing occurs.

As members of the bride of Christ, when we are unveiled and transparent, we allow others the priceless opportunity to be transformed into the image of God, reflecting His awesome love story. This happens when someone surrenders the truth of their struggle and another person can relate. It is as if a light is turned on in the darkness and we realize we are not alone. Christ is the source of light, and He desires to help and heal those who are lost in the darkness and suffering in isolation.

I have come to understand the power of transparency as I have opened up about my struggles through writing on my blog. I was hesitant to publish articles detailing the truth of who I am or the things my heart has believed. Yet each time I published an article, I heard about the brokenness of another woman as she thanked me for being real and for encouraging her that she is not alone. With God's help, I refused to hide the light of Christ and insisted on shining in this dark world. When people encounter hope like that, extraordinary things happen.

It starts within the hearts of each of us as we choose to turn to the Lord, just like a bride turns to her groom at the altar. It requires sacrifice and humility, the very things Jesus exemplified for us. When we lay down our lives at the altar, we acknowledge a purpose greater than ourselves.

A Word about Sex and True Intimacy

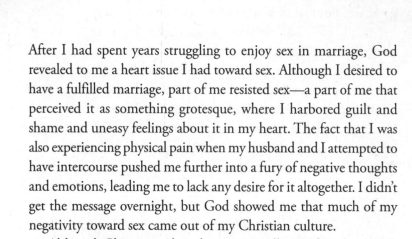

After I had spent years struggling to enjoy sex in marriage, God revealed to me a heart issue I had toward sex. Although I desired to have a fulfilled marriage, part of me resisted sex—a part of me that perceived it as something grotesque, where I harbored guilt and shame and uneasy feelings about it in my heart. The fact that I was also experiencing physical pain when my husband and I attempted to have intercourse pushed me further into a fury of negative thoughts and emotions, leading me to lack any desire for it altogether. I didn't get the message overnight, but God showed me that much of my negativity toward sex came out of my Christian culture.

Although Christian culture has meant well, too often the church has missed important opportunities to share what God's gift of sex is. The church has tried desperately to protect the younger generation from the world's sexual revolution, but as a whole has gone about it in a poor way. Instead of teaching age-appropriate lessons on God's beautiful design of sex, the church has chosen fear tactics, which have become ingrained in the minds of children, teens, and young adults with a terrifying *no!* The church is not fully responsible for teaching these topics; parents are definitely at fault for this too. In my opinion it should be a joint effort to share a positive message for those growing up today.

In addition to a large majority of young adults receiving the "absolute no" message about sex, the language surrounding the topic suppresses honest discussion when people avert using specific words such as *sex* or *intercourse*, as if they are ludicrous and dirty. When we do that, the piles of shame and guilt only grow higher and heavier!

By avoiding the conversation and substituting words like *intimacy* when referring to sex, not only are parents and/or the church allowing the world and its revolution to be the loudest voice teaching the young, but they inadvertently set the stage for young adults stepping into marriage to become unable to reconcile that sex is good and honorable, while missing out on true intimacy. Adults, my family included, preached abstinence, striking fear into my heart regarding pregnancy or STDs.

As much as I believe we *should* provide information about what can result from sex, I believe there is a greater message to be taught: God's great design of sex. We should not avoid a real conversation by simply offering a blatant *no!* sex rule. Instead it should be an open conversation about why sex was created, including the truth that sex is a good thing intended for a husband and wife to experience. (On a side note, I believe the no! message has also scared people away from embracing a healthy view of having children. I was terrified of having children, which also hindered my ability to embrace sex, because getting pregnant was taught more as a consequence, not as a blessing. Yet Psalm 127:3 says, "Children are a gift from the Lord.")

As I entered marriage, having lived a Christian life where I held strong convictions of sex being a no-no, it was difficult for me as a wife to embrace sex as a *yes!* It took time for me to even identify this as a problem. I was trained throughout impressionable years to avoid sexual intimacy, yet I was never trained how to properly cultivate it as a married woman, wisdom that should have been shared in a positive light, including when sex is appropriate and good.

Gradually God opened my eyes and my heart to this issue and

taught me how to rightfully define sex in marriage, as well as how to define true intimacy.

Sex was designed by God specifically for a husband and wife to experience. It is a physical *and* a spiritual act of two becoming one flesh. Science has proven God's perfect design of sex in that a husband was built with a strong desire to need it physically, while a wife needs the emotional benefits from it. As a husband and wife connect through sexual intimacy, they actually become addicted to each other, as the bond of love deepens and satisfies. God's design of sex comes with the freedom to be creative, but also has healthy boundaries to provide protection. Sex between a husband and wife is not a grotesque act, nor should it evoke shame or guilt. Sex is not a tool to use in marriage to get one's way, nor should it be unreasonably withheld. Sex is a beautiful gift that also includes wonderful benefits, such as relieving stress and satisfying a desire to draw near each other, and it has the potential of producing more gifts: children. Sex is a good thing, meant to be fulfilled and enjoyed within marriage.

God's design of sex has a richness that far exceeds my ability to expose and converse about in this book. Thankfully, other Christian leaders have been inspired to change the culture and attitude toward sex by producing amazing resources for married couples. The two greatest influences that helped reshape my view of sex while answering questions of boundaries were *No More Headaches* by Dr. Juli Slattery and *Real Marriage* by Mark and Grace Driscoll. God used these two books, as well as the Bible and conversations with close friends, to walk me through a process of unlearning the association of no with sex and teaching me what sex truly is.

❈ ❈ ❈

Simultaneously as God taught me about His great design of sex, He also taught me the importance of defining true intimacy. There is a deeply meaningful description of intimacy that has the power to radically transform marriages. Yet if we do not fully understand or grasp the meaning of this word, we miss out on it. Intimacy is a close and usually affectionate or loving personal relationship with another person.[10] Intimacy is making yourself known to another. It is being transparent with your feelings and thoughts, communicating them through conversation.

In my marriage, I have learned to do this as I practice talking to my husband, expressing to him what I know or what I experience. As I do that, my husband receives insight into who I am as a woman and as his wife. When either of us cultivates intimacy that way, the other person is almost always inspired to reciprocate, which reveals vulnerability as well as trust, a beautiful place for love to thrive.

Ultimately, I did not comprehend how to reveal certain parts about myself until I first encountered being unveiled before God. I had to recognize that my relationship with Him could go deeper, but to do so required me to let down walls in my heart, which terrified me. I resisted for a long time because I didn't know how to confront all the different issues that built those walls. Through prayer, I submitted myself to the Lord and asked Him to help me. I invited the Holy Spirit to show me how to draw closer to God in an intimate way and to transform the parts of me that were quick to keep Him at arm's length. I repented of the way I was, eager to be refined.

In that time I learned repentance was much more than just apologizing for all the wrong I had ever done; repentance was acknowledging my faults, failures, weaknesses, and sin, apologizing and then committing to change my ways, committing never to do those things again, and having faith that I could be redeemed, that I *could* change. Of course, at times I slipped into my old ways of selfishness, but each time the Holy Spirit convicted me and helped me to repent and turn from those ways. And every confrontation of repentance and grace made it easier to control my flesh while yielding to God. My character was being and still is being transformed into His image, into His character.

Once I overcame one area of weakness, it seemed another would be unveiled to me. I repeated the process of repentance in humility and in faith that I was becoming the woman God desired and I slowly began seeing my beauty, my worthiness, and my value—it was all wrapped up in my relationship with God and embracing His great love for me.

Intimacy with God is a holy experience of extraordinary encounters. Being unveiled before Him requires humility and vulnerability. I shared with God the deepest and darkest crevices in my heart, drawing my longings and hurts into His incredible light. Through prayer, whether as thoughts, spoken out loud, or written in my journal, I poured everything out and talked to Him. I pushed aside the notion that He already knew everything about me and willingly surrendered what I wanted Him to know, including my feelings, my past, my fears, and my dreams. Then I spent quality time reading His Word and listening for Him to respond. His words leapt off the pages of the Bible with authority and power, guiding me and affirming me in the direction He desired me to go. Some days I sang Him praises, while other days I wept in weariness. But no matter what my circumstances, I pursued God intentionally, maintaining my relationship with Him—and I haven't stopped.

❈　　❈　　❈

As I have pursued unveiling myself to God, He has never ceased revealing to me who He is. I feel as though I will never reach the summit of fully knowing Him, which I love. Acknowledging the heights and depths of God's love motivates a wild passion in my heart to seek after Him every day. I am intentionally intimate with the Lord as I pray, read His Word, worship, and submit to Him. Our relationship thrives because He has my attention and I have His. It's similar to what the lovers say in Song of Songs 6:3: "I am my lover's, and my lover is mine."

As you unveil yourself to God and pursue intimacy with Him,

you will discover great truths that will sustain you, such as recognizing Him as your everything. He will give you wisdom and guide you through every season you face. Instead of disappointment attacking you from unmet expectations, He will align your heart with His, shifting your perspectives heavenward. Instead of imperfections mounting and distorting the way you see yourself, you will accept the fact that Christ came to present you as radiant. Instead of fear crippling your frail body as you desperately yearn for security, He will be your refuge and your defender. Hope, confidence, and faith will rise in your heart, God's peace will give you the endurance to carry on, and His joy will be your strength. All the desires of your heart will be fulfilled when you turn to the Lord and allow Him to help you be unveiled and allow Him to align your heart with His.

❈ ❈ ❈

For every husband and wife, sex and intimacy will be a unique adventure. Some couples will have great sex, while others may battle in the bedroom or not have sex at all. I believe no matter what your love life is like, it is important to evaluate both sex and intimacy on a regular basis and assess whether there are areas that can be improved. The same is true for everyone's intimate relationship with God. Each of us will face different challenges in our relationships because we all have different areas of our character that need refining.

My husband and I struggled four long years, unable to have sex. However, in that time I learned a great deal about who I am and who God is, which I may never have acknowledged otherwise. Was it painful? Absolutely! Looking back, do I resent any of the pain? No! Why? Because I can say confidently that I know God—and to me that is everything! I also have a more profound knowledge of the mystery of marriage and how God uses marriage to make us holy. I would not be the woman I am today without what I have been through. My encouragement to you is to know that God will use all you have experienced and *will* experience for good.[11]

I am sympathetic to married couples who face conflict. The pain and injury inflicted through marriage can be brutal. If you are hurting, I encourage you to run to God and allow Him to mend your brokenness. This means you may have to confront some of your character traits that contribute to the conflict, and it may be challenging as God asks you to change, but He will help you along the way. He is the only One capable of healing you, strengthening you, and equipping you with what you need to thrive.

How the Environment May Affect You

Part of my unique story is that I am a wife who experienced excruciating pain during sex and found healing! Whether my physical healing was a miracle from God, a placebo effect from trying something new, or in fact a result of avoiding parabens, I cannot say with 100 percent certainty. I praise God first and foremost, and I believe all three had something to do with it. And while we may have found an answer to my body's mystery, there is still a lack of research and case studies to find a definitive harmfulness of parabens. I can say that I have also witnessed a rising cultural attentiveness to parabens. I found many awareness groups talking about the issue, as well as a trend of manufacturers advocating for "paraben-free" labeling.

Parabens may be approved by the FDA as a safe ingredient as long as only a small amount is included per product, but when you look at how many products contain parabens, as well as other potentially toxic ingredients, including BPA, phthalates, artificial dyes, and sulfates, it seems feasible that my body was being affected negatively. I hope that other women experiencing this problem are inspired to test whether these chemicals are a factor in their pain as well. (You can test by avoiding parabens for a given length of time and then evaluating your body for changes.)

And this is just one side effect. I cannot comprehend the other kinds of damage we have exposed our bodies to over the years through the ingredients we put in and on them. As a whole, we live in a world exposed to chemicals and elements interacting daily with our bodies, substances that have been crafted and altered by people.

All the negative impacts on our environment and our bodies are ultimately the result of sin. The enemy is actively pursuing many different avenues to destroy what God has made, and when any decisions are made motivated solely by profit and not through biblical principles or for the good of people, there are detrimental ripple effects.

My goal is not to pick on any one company or organization that might practice a process that harms our bodies, but rather I want to encourage you to look at the bigger picture: The enemy will use any means to viciously aggravate the foundation of your faith and your marriage.

A small exposure to a specific facial wash may not be significant enough to cause any real damage—or perhaps it could—but by examining the whole environment, it becomes obvious that our bodies are enduring a lot more than what we are fully aware of.

I never had a desire to buy "organic" anything or consider the ingredients in my personal care products until the Lord exposed the truth of how our sin affects more than just ourselves or our loved ones. When each of us makes a decision, we choose one of two mind-sets. My husband calls it "the conspiracy of evil" and says, "There are only two mind-sets in this world: that of Jesus Christ and that of the devil, and every person, whether knowingly or not, chooses to be of one mind or the other."

There is a conspiracy of evil occurring, and the mastermind behind such devastation is the devil. He seeks to kill, steal, and destroy the very creation that God loves so dearly, whether by destroying nature, our bodies, or our marriages. I caution you to be alert and aware of this conspiracy, and the truth that spiritual warfare happens more than just in the hearts of people. The enemy has wielded his practices for centuries as he manipulates people into making decisions that will ultimately affect everyone and everything in harmful ways through the environment. And if you and your husband have been experiencing contention because of physical issues, I strongly encourage you to research the world around you. I believe more marriages could be saved with this shift of perspective and discovery.

⊛   ⊛   ⊛

If you experience pain during intercourse, I want to validate your physical and emotional pain. I get it. And if I could wrap my arms around you right now, I would! Hang in there, friend, and never give up on God. This season of pain may be temporary or it may last a long time; only God knows. But if you can remain steadfast and faithful, God will be glorified. I hope some of the revelations God taught me, and that I shared in this book, will resonate with you and help you along your journey. I urge you to pay attention to ingredients in personal care products and avoid chemicals that could cause your body dysfunction. I also want to provide you with research I have stumbled across over the years, by introducing you to some medical terms, in hopes that you have an easier time understanding what you are experiencing—because when I was lost in how to find help for this issue, I felt so alone. Take your time in looking these things up, but be cautious in how you pursue your own research. Do not lean on your own wisdom to diagnose; rather let God lead you and be sure to discuss your findings with your doctor.

Terms for Women Who Experience Painful Intercourse

Dyspareunia: This is the medical term for painful intercourse, "which is defined as persistent or recurrent genital pain that occurs just before, during, or after intercourse."[12]

Vaginismus: When a woman's "muscle walls of the vagina con-
tract or spasm in response to attempted insertion. . . . This
involuntary muscle contraction can be mildly uncomfortable or
it may cause searing or tearing pain. Vaginismus can interfere
with normal activities like sex or getting a pelvic exam at the
doctor's office."[13]

Vaginitis: "Various conditions that cause infection or inflamma-
tion of the vagina. These conditions can result from a vaginal
infection caused by organisms such as bacteria, yeast, or viruses,
as well as by irritations from chemicals in creams, sprays, or even
clothing that is in contact with this area."[14]

Vulvodynia: "Affects the vulva, the external female genital organs.
This includes the labia, clitoris, and vaginal opening. Women with
vulvodynia have chronic vulvar pain with no known cause. Until
recently, doctors didn't recognize this as a real pain syndrome.
Even today, many women do not receive a diagnosis. They may
also remain isolated by a condition that is not easy to discuss.
Researchers are working hard to uncover the causes of vulvodynia
and to find better ways to treat it."[15]

Tips for Women Who Experience Painful Intercourse

- Talk to your doctor about it. Be sure there is no underlying
  issue such as an infection causing the pain.

- Use natural lubricants. Do your research and only use
  lubricants that do not contain chemicals that could
  potentially affect your body's natural function. Many
  lubricants unfortunately contain parabens. Invest in
  lubricants and other personal care products that do not
  contain toxic chemicals.

- During sex, switch positions. Use the freedom you have in marriage to adjust and acrobatically find a position that might be more comfortable.

- Communicate with your husband about your pain so that you can approach sex on the same page. Talk about what works and what doesn't.

- Communicate your pain with trusted friends to see if anyone else has experienced similar pain. Perhaps they have, and have remedies you have never thought of.

- Never stop praying and asking God to heal you! Pray in faith that He will heal you or show you what is causing the pain.

- Talk to yourself constantly, affirming yourself with positive thoughts. The brain is a powerful organ, and if anxiety is running rampant, it will be more challenging to relax enough for penetration.

- Initiate often. Don't always wait for your husband to heat things up. Most times the motivation to initiate inspires a positive outlook on the whole experience.

- Get your thyroid checked! It can definitely hinder your body's function. And if it is not in range, research natural remedies to help it balance out.

- Birth control can also play a role in affecting body chemistry. You may want to stop taking it to see if things improve, but allow several months as it takes a bit of time to get out of your system.

- Be patient as you engage with your husband. Don't give up too easily!

- Be mindful that diet and exercise affect your body's function and impact energy levels.

- Never stop investing in your marriage. Keep reading books or going to conferences with your husband. Discuss what you learn with each other and apply what you need!

Dear God,

Please bring healing to the woman struggling with painful intercourse. May You guide her to find the cause of her pain, and may You miraculously heal her. I pray against any threat of insecurity or anxiety when she attempts sexual intercourse. Please help her husband to be understanding about her body's function and help them to communicate about it openly and comfortably. I pray for her healing. In Jesus' name, amen!

APPENDIX D

The *Unveiled Wife* Blog

As God was teaching me about what it means to be unveiled and showing my husband and me how the environment can negatively affect our bodies, something beautiful was born. One day about a month after we experienced our healing, Aaron asked me, "Why don't you write our story?"

"What?" I asked, confused by his random question.

"You should start a blog and write our story as if you were writing in a journal. It might help you process what God is teaching you about our situation. And who knows, maybe another wife might find it helpful for her journey through marriage."

"No!" It shot out of my mouth quickly, before I actually thought it through. My response triggered me to stop and realize that I say no to my husband often. I didn't resist because his ideas were bad, I resisted because they scared me! "I'm not going to write about something that we are still working through ourselves. It was hard enough to live through it. I don't think I can handle going back to write it all out. It's just too fresh."

"I understand why you wouldn't want to do this," he said gently. "Just pray about it, okay?"

I agreed, reluctantly. I thought, *Why would I want to share my deepest, darkest pain for everyone to read?* I thought that was a little too unveiled!

But since I had promised Aaron, I did pray about the idea, and as I was beginning to pray, I felt an overwhelming peace about doing it. I was still hesitant, unsure if I could handle putting into words what we had gone through and what God was still teaching me. However, it was much easier saying no to my husband than to say no to God. So four months after we'd experienced healing and three months after Aaron's idea to start a blog, in February 2011 I told my husband I was ready to share our story.

"But if I'm going to do this, I need God's help. He will have to guide me in what to write. I want to explain what He is teaching me, and I want Him to be glorified."

"I agree with you and support you," he said.

I looked at Aaron's sweet face and realized again how he has always been my greatest supporter.

"Should we pray and dedicate this to God?"

I smiled, feeling excited. "Yes!"

Aaron prayed, "Dear Lord, we come before You, and we thank You for our marriage. Thank You for never forsaking us. Thank You for protecting our relationship and for healing us. Thank You for the good times and the hard ones. Please keep transforming our hearts so that we are more like You! I pray for my wife as she begins to share our story. Use this opportunity to help her process and reconcile all that we have been through. I pray her blog is read by other wives and that it encourages them to seek after You. Give her the words to write and bless her for doing this. We dedicate this to You. In Jesus' name, amen!"

Tears welled up as I listened to my husband pray. I was so grateful that he wanted the Lord to be glorified through this entire experience, that I could trust him, and that I knew he loved me and wanted to help others.

After he finished, I added, "Dear God, thank You for my husband, who never left me. Thank You for Your forgiveness and for pursuing me when I was angry toward You. Your love healed me and drew me back to You. Thank You for the friends we have made, the encouragement we have received, the miracle of sex, and for the courage to be transparent with each other. I pray a blessing over our marriage and ask that You continue to guard us against the enemy's attacks. Lord, I am terrified of writing our story. Please help me not to fear and remind me daily why I should do this. I pray this blog helps me in my role as a wife, but I also pray other wives will be encouraged. I submit this idea to You and ask that You lead me. In Jesus' name, amen."

⊛　⊛　⊛

With my husband's help, I began a blog to document my journey and transformation as a wife. I believed it would be therapeutic to write my journey as it was happening. I wanted to do this anonymously as I would be more easily and comfortably transparent. But as I prepared to start the blog, I felt God ask me to be real with who I am, to be unveiled.

The more I dwelt on the idea of being *unveiled*, the more passionate I became about using it in my blog to encourage other wives to embrace intimacy in their two most important relationships: with God and with their husbands. Aaron and I started brainstorming, and we landed on the name *Unveiled Wife*.

My first post, appropriately titled "The Introduction," explained that I would share parts of "my journey as a wife, unveiled, uncovered, and wide open, to purge my heart of the pain I have encountered and to encourage other women in the world who are, have been, or will soon be wives." I published it and the blog was officially launched March 11, 2011.

I did not know much about blogging. I had searched for others who were sharing their marriage stories, but to my surprise I could not find many. With trepidation, I wrote blog articles, hesitating every time I hit the publish button. Worry flooded my heart, wondering what people would think about me or my marriage. Once the articles were live I began receiving feedback almost immediately. I quickly realized there was a greater drought than my own—the world was thirsty for marriage encouragement.

After I posted that first piece, a woman named Jessica left a comment that confirmed to me what Aaron had believed—and God had prompted—all along:

> *Jen—*
> *You are such an inspiration! Thank you for creating a*
> *place where women know that they are not alone. You have*
> *created a place where we are understood and validated in*
> *our struggles, and you did this all through the glory of God!*
> *Truly amazing! We want more!*

With positive feedback building my confidence, I wrote another post, this time on my childhood, and received more comments. Mandy added:

> *Your blog was recommended to me by a friend, and I am*
> *already hooked. Your story parallels my own, which obviously*
> *intrigues me. I look forward to reading more, and all that*
> *you intend to bring to this virtual table. Thank you in*
> *advance for your raw honesty.*

God was showing me once again the power of transparency. As I opened my heart on my blog, others chimed in. Through the comments I received, God showed me the great need women had to be encouraged in their role as a wife. I wanted to reach through my articles and comfort each wife who read them. God was moving in extraordinary ways and He was using the pain I had endured for a purpose.

⊛　⊛　⊛

As I continued to write, my heart began to swell with a passion for marriage, especially as I gained more understanding about how the story of God's love for us is a direct correlation to marriage. I became fascinated with the establishment of marriage, the way God designed it, and how I could effectively use God's Word to draw from, as from a living well, for those who found my blog.

God was filling me with an insatiable devotion to help other marriages find freedom and fulfillment, a desire that has been growing ever since. I had stumbled upon a platform to share my struggles openly, hoping other wives would feel comfortable confronting theirs, abolishing the lie of embarrassment that taunts us all—the lie that says, *I am all alone.*

As much as it dented my pride to reveal my true nature, my character was able to mature because of my willingness to be transparent and vulnerable, rare qualities that are not often advocated by our society. Aaron and I may never have found the healing we received if we were not willing to be honest with each other and open with others—so I was committed to promoting that same transparency through *Unveiled Wife.*

With the attention my blog was gaining, many wives began asking if there was a similar blog for husbands. Aaron had already been praying about starting a blog of his own and responded to the expanding *Unveiled Wife* community by creating a virtual safe place for husbands. Two months after I began *Unveiled Wife*, he started *Husband Revolution*, calling men to step up in the responsibilities God has given them. Both of our blogs are being used daily to inspire married couples. Praise God!

In those first few months of blogging, my husband and I began to pray more earnestly for marriages around the world, gaining compassion for couples who were hurting like we were hurting. The *Unveiled Wife* and *Husband Revolution* blogs became havens for couples, places of encouragement and hope—the kind I wish we'd had early in marriage.

Since *Unveiled Wife* launched, God has grown it into a large community of wives connecting from all over the world. *Unveiled Wife* has blossomed into an amazing ministry with some unique categories, including Prayer of the Day, Marriage Resources, Letter to My Husband, and Letters to Celebrity Wives. I am still in awe of God's grace and the transformation He is making in me by His grace working through me to be able to serve such a phenomenal group of women. Wives—whether they are hurting or rejoicing— are coming together through *Unveiled Wife* to uplift one another as they experience the awesome gift and mystery of marriage.

Allowing God to use me as a vessel to share His love story with other wives has blessed me in amazing ways. From receiving stories of atheists sharing my articles on Facebook to discovering that women in rural parts of Africa and the Philippines are reading them and being encouraged, it makes me want to share more. I am humbled by the comments and e-mails I receive from the women in the *Unveiled Wife* community, proclaiming the good happening as a result of my obedience.

I also benefit from the articles I write as they keep me accountable to fulfill my role as a God-fearing wife, for I cannot possibly offer any wisdom if I am not applying it myself! As much as I make it a priority to practice what I preach, there are times when I fail. However, when I am honest with the community about my weakness, I've found that it strengthens us all the more, as others can use my experience to evaluate their lives, all while we pray and affirm one another to press on. Transparency is the greatest attribute of *Unveiled Wife*, and it is that raw honesty that draws hearts in and closer to God. My articles also remind me daily to pursue God and keep *my* relationship with Him my greatest priority. *Unveiled Wife* is a beautiful place where I have seen the body of Christ support and edify one another as we are encouraged to submit to God. I am so grateful for my husband's suggestion and that I listened. Out of our pain, not only have I found the blog to be therapeutic for me as I continue to work through marriage issues, but it has also birthed a ministry that I never would have dreamed possible.

I WOULD LOVE TO CONNECT WITH YOU!

All you have to do is text
#unveiledwifebook
to (737) 777-9433.

As soon as you sign up, I'll send you some additional
exclusive content, questions, and encouragement.
I'll also send you *The Unveiled Wife
Daily Prayer* via e-mail.

I'm so honored to connect with you in this way, and
I really hope that this will be a blessing to you!

HAVE ME COME SPEAK

Marriage conferences, women's retreats,
church events, or MOPS groups

Send speaking inquiry to Booking@unveiledwife.com.

CP0878

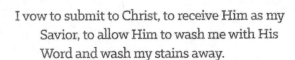

Vows of an unveiled wife

I vow to submit to Christ, to receive Him as my Savior, to allow Him to wash me with His Word and wash my stains away.

I vow to lay down my expectations of marriage and seek God's will above all else.

I vow to be sanctified, to allow God to reveal sin in my life and to repent of it.

I vow to live by faith, to let go of my insecurities and trust God.

I vow to love and respect my husband with my words and my actions.

I vow to pursue true intimacy with God and my husband.

I vow to be continually unveiled before God, my husband, and others so that Christ will be glorified.

I do.

The Unveiled Wife by Jennifer Smith. #unveiledwifebook

But whenever
someone turns
to the Lord
the veil is
taken away.

2 CORINTHIANS 3:16

The Unveiled Wife by Jennifer Smith. #unveiledwifebook

Acknowledgments

Dear God, thank You for saving me. Thank You for unveiling me. I am in awe of Your extraordinary love and Your amazing grace. Thank You for the beautiful gift of marriage, and thank You for my marriage. Thank You for using so many different people to reveal Yourself to me. Because of You, my marriage is reconciled and I am able to share about it. I love You, Father! Amen!

Aaron, you are an incredible man. Thank you for enduring through the drought, carrying me when I couldn't walk, and loving me when I was unlovable. You have my heart!

Eliott, I cannot explain how much joy you bring to my life. Your presence is a daily reminder of God's goodness, grace, and glory. You are going to be an awesome big brother soon!

Tom and Heidi, best friends, the first example we witnessed of raw honesty. Your marriage is a blessing to others as you invite people in and walk with them along the journey. Thank you for leading us.

Chris and Joanne, God's hands and feet, God's heart—He extended His grace through you. Your humility is honorable and your passion for God's love story has changed me. Thank you for advising us and for encouraging me to step out in faith, believing what God was capable of when I was weak.

Bill and Michelle, ambassadors for Him, you lavished us with love and gave us an opportunity to thrive. Keep shining, for God is changing lives through you!

Matt and Lisa, dear mentors and agent, words cannot describe the deep appreciation I have for you both as you have showed confidence and support in the message I share through *The Unveiled Wife*. As a team you have helped me fulfill my passion for writing and have inspired me to trust God in all areas of my life.

Parents and family, I wouldn't be who I am without each of you. I value the relationships we have, and I am grateful for all that we have experienced together.

Craig and Corrin, selfless servants, thank you for being obedient to God's call and showing me God's love. I love you forever.

Nathan and Daisy, best friends, thank you for helping us laugh and experience joy when life was burdensome.

Dale and Veronica, best friends, we appreciate the love, support, and encouragement for marriage and blogging.

Dear friends—you all know who you are—thank you for doing life with us. The impact and influence you have made on our hearts has contributed to the marriage we have today. We love you!

Unveiled Wife contributors, friends, and wives in this wonderful community, my heart is in a constant state of prayer for you. Thank you for supporting this ministry by affirming me with your words and sharing it with others. You are significant.

The Tyndale team, you rock! I appreciate all the hard work you poured into making this story become available to so many women! Thank you for taking such good care of us. You are family!

Ginger, my phenomenal editor, thank you for taking the time to draw out of my heart what God wanted to share all along. Your grueling questions and gentle demands to help me through the process of writing this story refined it in a way I am so grateful for.

Kimberly and Catherine, my high school teachers, you taught me the importance of doing things well. You befriended me when I was young and impressionable, encouraging me to fulfill my dreams. Your impact as teachers still touches my heart.

Notes

1. Excerpted from a presentation called "God's Glory in Marriage" by Paul Washer, John Piper, and Voddie Baucham. For this portion by Paul Washer, see 3:38–5:20 of https://www.youtube.com/watch?v=ZACkRe_W4Gg.
2. Carolyn C. Ross, "Overexposed and Under-Prepared: The Effects of Early Exposure to Sexual Content," *Psychology Today*, http://www.psychologytoday.com/blog/real-healing/201208/overexposed-and-under-prepared-the-effects-early-exposure-sexual-content.
3. Dan Goldman, "Survey Shows Students as Victims and Perps of Cyber Crime," *Messenger Post*, June 20, 2008, http://www.rit.edu/news/utilities/pdf/2008/2008_06_20_RushHenriettaPost_Survey_Cyber_Crime_McQuade.pdf.
4. *Merriam-Webster Online*, s.v. "intimacy," http://www.merriam-webster.com/dictionary/intimacy.
5. *Merriam-Webster Online*, s.v. "intimate," http://www.merriam-webster.com/dictionary/intimate.
6. The website of The American Medical Association, http://www.ama-assn.org/ama/pub/physician-resources/patient-education-materials/atlas-of-human-body/endocrine-system.page.
7. "Parabens," US Food and Drug Administration, October 31, 2007, http://www.fda.gov/cosmetics/productsingredients/ingredients/ucm128042.htm#What_are_parabens.
8. Gary Thomas, *Sacred Marriage* (Grand Rapids: Zondervan, 2000), 89.
9. "The Holy of Holies and the Veil," The Tabernacle Place, http://the-tabernacle-place.com/articles/what_is_the_tabernacle/tabernacle_holy_of_holies.
10. Dictionary.com, s.v. "intimacy," http://dictionary.reference.com/browse/intimacy.
11. "We know that God causes everything to work together for the good of those who love God and are called according to his purpose for them" (Romans 8:28).
12. Mayo Clinic Staff, "Diseases and Conditions: Painful Intercourse (Dyspareunia)," the website of Mayo Clinic, January 25, 2012, http://www.mayoclinic.org/diseases-conditions/painful-intercourse/basics/definition/con-20033293.
13. "Women's Health: Vaginismus," *WebMD*, http://www.webmd.com/women/guide/vaginismus-causes-symptoms-treatments (accessed November 2014).
14. "Women's Health: Vaginal Infections, *WebMD*, http://www.webmd.com/women/guide/sexual-health-vaginal-infections.
15. "Women's Health: Vulvodynia: Causes, Symptoms, and Treatments," *WebMD*, http://www.webmd.com/women/guide/vulvodynia.

About the Author

By God's grace, Jennifer Smith created *Unveiled Wife*, a web-based ministry for wives, in March 2011. She publishes weekly marriage articles including encouragements, devotions, and prayers of the day, all geared toward empowering wives. A large part of Jennifer's ministry for *Unveiled Wife* is done via Facebook, Twitter, Instagram, and Pinterest, where she leads a community of wives from all around the world.

Jennifer is passionate about encouraging wives through the journey of marriage. She has served in ministry alongside her husband, traveling as missionaries to Zambia, Malawi, Canada, and Nicaragua. Jennifer and her husband have been married seven years and live in central Oregon with their young son.

MORE FROM
THE UNVEILED WIFE

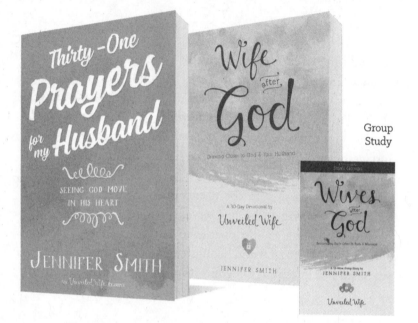